Strategy for Triumph
A Christian Perspective on Problems

Strategy for Triumph
A Christian Perspective on Problems

Rick C. Howard

Naioth Sound and Publishing
Woodside, California

Unless otherwise indicated, all Scripture quotations are taken from *The New King James Version* of the Bible.

Strategy for Triumph: A Christian Perspective on Problems
ISBN 0-9628091-1-X
Copyright © 1991 by Rick C. Howard
Naioth Sound and Publishing
2995 Woodside Road, Suite 400
Woodside, CA 94062
U.S.A.

Published by Naioth Sound and Publishing
2995 Woodside Road, Suite 400
Woodside, CA 94062
U.S.A.

Cover design and book production by
DB & Associates Design Group, Inc.
P.O. Box 52756
Tulsa, OK 74152

"Where Am I Going"
(Cy Coleman, Dorothy Fields)
© 1965, 1969 Notable Music Co., Inc. & Lida Enterprises, Inc.
All rights administered by WB Music Corp.
All rights reserved. Used by Permission.

Dedication

To my mother, my wife,
and my daughter, who have lovingly
nurtured and supported me
in the struggle of my being.

CONTENTS

Oh, No!
Not Another Christian
Self-Help Book!

There has to be a bit of egotist in anyone who writes a book. What makes any of us think that he has truly solved a mystery or discovered an infallible formula? And what's even more, who dares to believe that anyone else truly cares what we think, or certainly how we feel?

Perhaps, in essence, we finally write to satisfy some inner compulsion, more for our peace than others' pleasure. Who really knows? Another book, another era, and with it the ever-present possibility that the author will one day wish the unmerciful honesty of print had never captured his spirit or bound his thoughts!

Nowhere does one come more reluctantly to print than in the ruthless vulnerability of the evangelical community. Opinion here is sacred, or at least *ex cathedra*. Belief is woven all too tightly into the fabric of personhood, although its criteria at least must change, enlarge, and even occasionally die. And the teacher is his message, we are told.

Seldom, if ever, does the opportunity exist for the "trial balloon," the developing theory, or the tentative hypothesis.

Rejecting the Fences

Perhaps I write, more than anything else, to reject those fences altogether. I have found answers helpful, but seldom complete, and I take them as they are. I joy in incompletion and struggle as a representative dynamic of God's ever-changing creation.

I am, myself, a mixture — a combination of heaven and earth — in love with God and falteringly pursuing holiness, but all too obviously alive in a body not yet redeemed.

I cannot entirely agree with Bonhoeffer that grace can only be the sum and not the data of life's equation. Christian experience is adventure; more trial and error than settled boundaries and fixed equations. That implies no uncertainty on the unchangeables, but simply pure and sacred mystery on the majority of the issues with which we are faced.

No Simple Answers

So on we go, if reading past this page is plausible. The pages are more hope than help. I don't think there are simple answers to most Christian dilemmas. These are more sign-posts than hypotheses, and they call more honestly for perusal than persuasion.

If they help you, then I'm glad. If they don't, I'm still glad they're written. Socrates once said, purportedly, that the unexamined life was not worth living.

L'chaim! Here's to life — examined life!

Rick C. Howard

Woodside, California
January 1991

FOREWORD

It was a timely treat for me to be able to read Rick Howard's most recent book, *Strategy for Triumph: A Christian Perspective on Problems.* Rick has avoided theological cliches, psychological "buzz words," and religious generalities. Someone once stated, "Pat answers are an enemy of progress." Rick has certainly stayed away from "pat answers."

Another thing that impressed me about this book is how Rick avoided the two extreme positions regarding human pain and Christian suffering.

At one end of the religious spectrum is the "Pollyanna" gang. Their concepts about Christians include winning popularity contests, making it into the Top 10, being queen of the ball, or becoming the star athlete. These people act like life is one big hundred-yard dash to heaven's rewards: "Give your life to Jesus and it's glory all the way!" Rick's message doesn't fall into that category.

The other extreme Rick has avoided is the message of the "suffering cult." Some church groups teach that suffering has redemptive value. In other words, what Jesus suffered in His crucifixion wasn't enough to save us. We have to *add* to His plan of redemption by suffering some ourselves. He didn't do enough to save us, according to this thinking, so any suffering we do makes "Brownie points" for eternity.

The thing that is deadly about the suffering cult is that it takes us right back to Cain, who wanted to be accepted by the efforts of his own hands. Rick deals with suffering, but avoids the idea that our suffering is redemptive.

Quoting Rick, he has this evaluation of the human arena as it affects the Christian believer: "Problems become the context for change and therefore for release, advance, and growth."

I was impressed with his advice for troubled people to recognize that God has a practical discipline for everyone. Submitting to His plans for our life can eliminate a lot of petty chaffing, and irritating, bugging circumstances, according to Rick. If you have a pressure point and want to work through it, I suggest you read Rick's book and catch his progressive message.

Sow a thought — reap an idea.
Sow an idea — reap an action.
Sow an action — reap a habit.
Sow a habit — reap a character.
Sow a character — reap a destiny.

—Anonymous Author

Dick Mills

CHAPTER ONE

The Problem With Problems

Charlie Brown, infamous "Everyman" of the 20th century, once said to his sidekick, Linus, "We critical people are always being criticized."

Christian life is rampant with trials because it is, in essence, a probation itself, incomplete, transient, and "going somewhere."

Therefore, the nature of the experience is a problem with problems. Not necessarily trouble, external persecution, or martyrdom (at least in its more obvious forms), but more often the crises of personhood which are meant to be faced for the pure joy of their mystery and the clear hope of their solution.

In another enigmatic Charles Schulz comic strip, our friend and life-identity partner, Linus, is shown building a marvelous, carefully sculptured sand castle on a sunny beach.

Subsequent frames of the strip show first drops, then sheets, and finally torrents of rain multiplying in almost apocalyptic fashion, until the sand castle is destroyed.

The one and only conversation balloon is in the final frame, with Linus saying, "There's a lesson to be learned in this somewhere, but I don't know what it is."

Problems Are Not Negative

Problems are not negative. Ask a scientist, technician, or mathematician! Problems are the substance of career, the meaning to existence, and the reason for being. They start adrenalin flowing and the mind working.

Problems are to life what exercise is to the body: They heighten ability, strengthen endurance, enlarge capacity and, as they are faced and resolved, lengthen the quality and, more likely, the quantity of our life.

Ask a person who exercises regularly. No one feels like facing the push-ups, jogging, or weightlifting. But when they're done, life takes on a clarity and excitement never available to the armchair spectator of a football match!

The discipline of fasting is much the same: It is not so much the process as it is the fulcrum of the fast itself. Something is being addressed worth sacrifice. The eyes brighten, the pace quickens, and clarity abounds.

Enjoy Your Problems!

Therefore, you should joy in the abundance of your problems, as to growth in a relationship. Development is proportional; pity those who are not inundated with problems!

It can reasonably be argued from the New Testament records that participation is the very crux of maturity. Conversely, the perpetually immature demand their experience vicariously.

What else is "milk," so adamantly attacked as an ongoing Christian diet by Paul in Corinthians and by the writer to the Hebrews, if not an overdependency on that which has passed through the digestive system of another?

Solid food, according to Hebrews 5, belongs to the fully mature, and demands skill in the word of righteousness and personal partaking. But look at its rewards!

The perceptions and senses are exercised (the very word in the original Greek is *gumnazo*) in the ultimate characteristic of maturation — discernment and discrimination.

The Word of God, a microcosm of the Christian life itself, abounds with problems which must be faced, researched, examined, accepted, and ultimately embraced to be understood.

2

It is, in fact, semantically reassuring to know that the very word "problem" comes from a Greek verb and preposition combined, *problema,* which can be translated "a throwing forward, or casting forward."

The Problem With Problems

The problem with problems is that they can no more be ignored than warts or hemorrhoids! Problems point to themselves. They draw attention to an issue yet to be faced, an understanding needing to be reached, or an area yet to be exposed.

Problems are not an arena of the erratic or the unexpected. They are as much the norm to growth as food and water are to life.

Daylight-type problems can be faced with one of two declarations: "Good *Lord,* morning!" or "Good morning, Lord!" My spirit can have a sense of anticipation or distress, expectation or disquiet: "Oh, yes, here it is — another problem to be solved," or "Oh, no, not another problem!"

Fifty Years Repeated Forty Times

A contemporary New Testament scholar has said that his studies have revealed three reoccurring misemphases in the history of the Christian Church. (In reality, there haven't been two thousand years of Church history — only fifty years repeated forty times!)

These three misemphases are actually fatal mixtures which periodically poison the pot of Christian teaching, and have done so since the first century. No one doubts that diversity is strengthening, but such a mixture is, in fact, devastating.

First is a compromise on the sovereign and exalted nature of God. In whatever form this takes — from the works-salvation of early Church centuries, called Pelagianism, to the Christian-humanism of today — it is always an emphasis on the *practical sovereignty* of God.

3

A. W. Tozer once wrote, "Low views of God destroy the Gospel for all those that hold them." Needless to add, if God is viewed primarily as One who gives us what we *want*, or what we decide in our finite wisdom that we *need*, we are buying into an incredibly low view of God.

Second is a weakened stance concerning the completed and final revelation of holy Scriptures. We must not succumb either to a fatal "bibliolatry," or join distracting verbal battles on semantic differences concerning "inspiration."

Never doubt the subtle and dangerous poison of elevating fresh or new words and contemporary "revelation knowledge" to equality with the holy and completed Word of God!

"The Present Truth"

Each succeeding revival movement has been tempted to contend for a "present truth" which would, in fact, *alter* or *amplify* the writing of the Scriptures.

There was a second century Christian error called Montanism which did this. We must not allow a received new "word" to compromise the completion of the Scripture or true biblical authority.

"But what of problems?" you ask. "You promised a clear, fresh, examined life." And so I did. The reoccurring mixtures above contribute and lead to a heresy that is long-range in its effect and imperatively pertinent to our study.

The "Here-and-Now" Kingdom

The *third* mixture is the error which modifies a pure and biblical perspective of the nature and the essence of the Christian life. In this misemphasis, the kingdom of God is perceived as discovered in *this* world and by the things we possess. Thus, "here and now" becomes the all-important criteria for Christian achievement.

It is a utilitarianism which centers on the good of man and the quality of a current life experience. Like Early Church Gnosticism, man's specific spiritual pilgrimage is denied. The flesh-spirit struggle and sojourn is repudiated. Suffering in no way, by this teaching, is to be connected with Christian experience. This repudiation exhibits a western prosperity which wastes, consumes, and never seems to learn.

In light of the clear teachings of Paul, James, Peter, and the ultimate Teacher, Jesus, it is no wonder anyone holding to such ideas must broaden and change the completed Scriptures.

When Problems Make Sense

Now you can see the problem with problems! They only make sense within a framework of growth and change. Have you, for example, lived in a family where a young man or a young woman was reaching puberty? Each new sign of development — pubic hair, added height, or reproductive process — was greeted with enthusiasm. Never mind that there was uncertainty and acne; the individual was becoming a man or a woman!

This does not, of course, minimize the difficulty and even the danger of a transition period. Such periods, it seems to me, are always fraught with both danger and delight. Is that not the reason why the writer to the Hebrews described some believers as producing fruit of righteousness and receiving profit from chastisement, while others became profane and missed the blessing?

looking diligently lest anyone fall short of the grace of God; lest any root of bitterness springing up cause trouble, and by this many become defiled.

Hebrews 12:15

I have a real problem understanding problems if I deny the essential nature and essence of the Christian life. If I am to measure success or acceptance in the Christian experience by the *absence* of problems, or conversely by the *presence* of material blessings, I am left with a multitude of Christian dilemmas.

5

"The Sufferings of This Present Time"

There simply cannot be logical Christian theology if one denies the transitory and probational nature of the believer's earthly existence.

The joys, blessings, and prosperity of this life are but a sip of the ultimate commensurate cup of the Father's provision for eternity. Similarly, "...the sufferings of this present time are not worthy to be compared with the glory which shall be revealed in us" (Romans 8:18).

"Otherworldliness!" you gasp. "Pure, unadulterated pie-in-the-sky someday theology!"

Not quite. The issue is context, not compromise. As Paul explains it in the teaching of resurrection, "If in this life *only* we have hope in Christ, we are of all men the most pitiable" (1 Corinthians 15:19; italics added).

This was the quandary of David, Job, and Job's so-called friends. God's payday is not always Friday. Christian victory cannot be measured by how many Jacuzzis you have in your bathrooms or how many Mercedes you have in your garage!

A predominance of problems, even the exponential multiplication of them, most often marks important transition. As Bruce Larson so well developed the theme in *Living on the Growing Edge*, this hard, frightening, insecure edge of new learning is an exciting framework for growth and change.

But one must always leave the secure, the knowable, and the comfortable for a Canaan of mystery and danger. Real faith always means leaving secure old agendas and venturing forth, as Abraham, not knowing where you are going.

Our Pilgrim Experience

Christian experience — the faith life in general — is to live provisionally with no earthly city. Abraham's priority of "pitching tents" — living simply and provisionally in the "now" — and "building altars" — concentrating on the eternal and the spiritual — is the priority experience of every true believer.

As one writer commented, "Our difficulty at the Judgment seat of Christ will not be with passports, but with baggage. That is the way it usually is when one travels."

Almost all of us can look back to our clumsy, embarrassing transition to adolescence and recognize, through the 20-20 vision of hindsight, how strategically the imagined "problems" were intricately woven into the fabric of exciting new changes and ultimate maturation.

*Man*opause: Midlife Crisis

But try that pattern on during the disruption of menopause, or its more tragic and generally internalized, *man*opause. The midlife crisis is an epidemic level of experience which results in untold loss of energy and effectiveness in our society. Many people never recover.

A *Wall Street Journal* article some years ago described this loss with the deceptive headline, "How To Retire at 35." It described the people who drag on for another thirty years until reaching official retirement age, but who have given up long ago, ceasing to function creatively and meaningfully.

The article went on to say that the more fortunate ones in that situation were fired, which forced them to come to grips with who and what they were. They were thus enabled to start over, often in a new career, but always with fresh energy and direction.

I think my *man*opause was the longest in recorded history! I awoke one morning at age thirty-eight and began mourning that I hadn't written the great American book, wasn't involved in the romantic ideal I had dreamed of for marriage or family, and was only a mediocre success in my career.

I was, so to speak, out standing in left field. My drooping continued almost to my forty-second birthday, and had it continued another six months, I might well have lost my wife, what friends remained, and what was left of my career!

Crisis: Collision!

What is this crisis? It is, in fact, the collision of life-realities with the external agendas we accepted in post-adolescence and had spent our remaining years serving. Those external agendas, generally accepted between sixteen and twenty, are the simplistic "what" agenda that finds expression in attainment, popularity, and success.

Their disillusionment and failure, as life-threatening as it may seem are, in fact, the opening of the door for a truer and more exciting internal agenda based on "who I am" and "what my gifts are."

Tragically, the materialistic emphasis of western civilization and culture postpones the true emphases until midlife, and even then they are only perceived in crises.

The more committed to where we have been and the more defensive we are about the things we have spent our life doing, the least apt we are to truly change.

A "Fresh and Fragrant" Dimension

How much wasted time there is in rationalizing and defending ourselves, when openness to reevaluation and the process of change is a true dynamic for life. Here again, the problem is the opportunity for being thrust forth into an entirely fresh and fragrant dimension of being. It is again the *problema* in problem — the being *cast forward* that we must always be willing to see.

Our son Chip was only two. He had played all morning on his plastic-wheeled scooter, ramming merrily about our California bungalow. I enjoyed watching him and listening to his untranslatable conversation with himself and anyone or anything around.

For some reason, the tricycle turned over as he maneuvered from our bedroom into the hall. No big deal. He'd already survived a host of such crises. But this time the rear wheels had mysteriously lodged against the frame of the bedroom door. He pulled and fussed to right his toy, totally

8

unaware that he was, by simple physics, pulling against the combined support of the entire wall and, in fact, the whole house.

I watched, amused, as he spoke in angry, frustrated tones, and twice sat down for a bit of a cry. Tears more of frustration and anger than hurt or sorrow poured from his eyes. Each time he got up to try again — pulling, jabbering, and crying.

"Get Me Out of This Mess!"

Finally, for some reason, he looked up and saw me standing there. I shall never forget the look in his eyes. "Well, Dad, don't just stand there!" he seemed to say, motioning and gesturing about his plight. "Get me out of this mess."

I reached down, attempting to show him the problem by pulling the wheels away from the door jam so he could right the vehicle himself. He was totally oblivious to the elementary lesson in physics. Without so much as a salute or "thank you," he was off again on the business of his journey.

We are all consummately like my son — more frustrated and angry than learning or listening when the seemingly ceaseless door jams of life stop our progress or halt our efforts to get on with "business as usual."

We are, more importantly, terribly upset at the apparent unconcern of the heavenly Father to our plight; upset and unheeding when He lovingly attempts to teach us through our strife.

"I've been there," I thought that morning, as I watched my son. "Why can't I ever learn?"

CHAPTER 2

What Is A Christian?

There are few of us who did not come to a rude awakening after marriage when we began living out the realities of two persons becoming one. Too often the problem was "which one?" and the solution seemed impossible and schizophrenic.

I will not perform a marriage until I have had several counseling sessions with the couple. In essence, I try to talk the prospective bride and bridegroom *out* of getting married to begin with!

I want their expectations and desires to be of the utmost in honesty and considered judgment. But couples inevitably come through the sessions and get married anyway.

Often as I repeat the ceremony, asking the self-conscious, insecure bridegroom, "Will you forsake all others, endow her with your worldly goods, and keep her in sickness and in health?" and I hear the man say, "I do, I do," I can almost hear him think, "Let's get this over with!"

I have afterwards wanted to grab him by the bow tie and say, "Hey, turkey! Do you know what you just *said?*" (That should get a rise out of the wedding witnesses!) But, of course, he doesn't have the foggiest idea what he is saying in most instances.

What can he know of the changed existence of this person as life crises come one by one? He doesn't know what he is saying, but he will soon enough. That's life. It takes us at

11

our word and proceeds to live out its promise and potential. It's not unfair; it's the arena for growth and maturity.

Similarly, does anyone know in reality what he is doing when he confesses and believes "Jesus Christ is Lord"? I doubt it. He has come, as it were, to the door of salvation guilt-ridden and empty, burdened and needy.

The Invitation of a Lifetime

The words "Whosoever will may come" seem like the invitation of a lifetime, and the conditions of belief in Christ's atoning salvation and confession of His Lordship seem trivial but necessary details. And then, by faith — by this confession — one walks into the glory of a newfound life.

It is rare for there not to be a temporary *"whoopee session"* in which the new convert seems deliriously happy, fulfilled, and free! But that is the unreality of asking the bridegroom during the honeymoon, "How's married life?"

No one can understand the problems in the Christian life from a simplistic look at conversion, any more than one can understand the ultimate process of marriage from the celebration at a reception!

Origins are seldom ultimates. The place of understanding a believer's problems must frame itself from an answer to the ultimate question, "What is a Christian?" The nature and essence of the biblical believer's life is the only true explanation for "Why this or that happens or is allowed to Christians."

Who knows when it happens? At some point, inside the door of Christian experience, the Holy Spirit stops the "whoopee" of a new convert and lovingly guides him to see the inside lintel of the door he came through.

The Family Secret Is Revealed

Remember, its simple outside promise was "Whosoever will may come." But inside is written the family secret, made known only to the born again.

...He chose us in Him before the foundation of the world, that we should be holy and without blame before Him in love,

having predestined us to adoption as sons by Jesus Christ to Himself, according to the good pleasure of His will,

to the praise of the glory of His grace, by which He has made us accepted in the Beloved.

Ephesians 1:4-6

Christian life, in other words, is *God's choice*, and its determination is at His direction. Now that's another issue entirely! It is both exciting and frightening.

Salvation is God's idea. I was not saved only to have my sins forgiven, my burdens lifted, and to secure a guaranteed, reserved seat in a blessed eternity. Salvation has brought me into a perspective of purpose found only in God's will and pleasure.

Predestined to Conformity

The Apostle Paul so adequately captured its fulfillment by saying, "For whom He foreknew, He also predestinated to be conformed to the image of His Son, that He might be the firstborn among many brethren" (Romans 8:29).

Conformity to anything is a process. Watch a gardener shaping a hedge, or a sculptor forming a statue. In salvation, it's as though the Holy Spirit points the young believer down an athletic field and says, "Do you see those goal posts? That's where you're headed. It's tough to get there. Around the door of the entrance to the Christian experience there are wall-to-wall believers. But strike out toward that goal and the crowd thins out! There's a world of helps for you, but only you can determine the pace of progress. Well, it's up to you. Get started."

That truth is confirmed by life in general. Dynamic life is always life in progress toward specifically defined goals. The likeness of Jesus Christ is a specific, attainable modeled experience.

It isn't cloud nine, ethereal, or flimsy. The Scriptures reveal the true model in the vulnerable, incarnate life and action of Jesus Christ, God's Son, our Savior and Lord.

Having the Mind of Christ

Paul writes:

Let this mind be in you which was also in Christ Jesus,

who, being in the form of God, did not consider it robbery to be equal with God,

but made Himself of no reputation, taking the form of a servant, and coming in the likeness of men.

And being found in appearance as a man, He humbled Himself and became obedient to the point of death, even the death of the cross.

Philippians 2:5-8

This "mind" we are to possess is, in this instance, a present active imperative of the Greek *phroneo*, a word conveying the strongest suggestion of "right-minded, intelligent, continuing mental attitude."

We might more accurately translate Philippians 2:5 as, "Have the same right-minded attitude which Christ had."

Greek scholars remind us that *phroneo* was often attached to first-century wills and testaments, somewhat like "Being of sound mind" is used today. *Phroneo* means, basically, "taking sides" in an intelligent and fully considered matter. It is a verb of the strongest possible action.

What, then, is the likeness or image of Jesus Christ to which our entire believing experience is directed? A clue comes from the direction of Jesus' right-minded, fully considered choice.

He took upon Himself the form of a bond slave, *doulos*, in order to wholly meet the Father's purpose. Again, the New Testament Greek is specific. *"Being* in the form of God" (verse 6) is the word *morphe*, "an outward display of unchangeable essence or substance."

14

"The Form of a Servant"

Jesus Christ always was and will be divine. But, says verse seven, He took upon Himself the form of a servant. In this verse the word "form" is from *schema*, "the changeable but, nonetheless real, outward appearance," such as the stages of development from childhood to adolescence to adulthood.

Clearly, then, the believer is to accept a right-minded attitude, the same as Jesus, which was a realistic acceptance of a temporary or probationary relationship as a bond slave.

In other words, the believer "in the likeness of Jesus" is a bond servant of Christ as He was, in all things, the bond servant of the Father.

Surely that point is self-explanatory. "The works I do," He said, "the words I speak, are all the Father's. The glory and purpose is the Father's."

In fact, Philippians 2:8 declares, "And being found in appearance as a man, He humbled Himself and became obedient to the point of death, even the death of the cross."

The Believer's Trademark

Without question, humility and obedience were, for both Christ and His disciples, the obvious trademarks of believers' servanthood.

Do you remember the remarkable conversation between Jesus and the woman at the well? When the disciples returned with food from the village, the Lord's response to them was, "I have food to eat of which you do not know" (John 4:32).

The word "food" in this verse refers to the process of sustaining life by eating, not a description of what was eaten. We could easily translate Jesus' statement as, "I have a process for sustaining true life which you haven't discovered."

One might imagine Peter saying to his compatriots, "When did McDonald's open in Samaria?" Actually, he or someone asked, "Has anyone brought Him anything to eat?" (verse 33).

Jesus answered, "My food (that which sustains my life) is to do the will of Him who sent Me, and to finish His work" (verse 34).

Notice carefully an important truth: A bond slave is not a hired servant; he is irrevocably and unconditionally united to the will and purpose of the master. "I am sustained," Jesus here revealed, "by the obedient fulfillment of my purpose."

I can hear it now. Some reader will argue indignantly, "But Jesus said, 'I call you servants no longer, but friends'"! And, of course, you're correct. It is just as correct to quote the Father as He spoke from heaven, saying, "This is my beloved Son, in whom I am well pleased."

Servanthood is probationary. It is a sensible, right-minded response to the mercy, grace, and relationship God makes available. It is a *schema*, a changeable form, not the unchangeable or essential essence.

Jesus took this mental attitude with full knowledge of its ultimate cost, in order that the higher good and resplendent glory of the Father might be realized. He was always a Son, and so are those born again of the Spirit.

Total Self-Renunciation

But He "emptied Himself," or "made Himself of no reputation" (Philippians 2:7). This is the aorist active indicative of a Greek word *keinon*, meaning "to empty, or to make empty." The word "Himself" in the sentence is emphatic. This is an extremely graphic expression of the totality of the self-renunciation of Jesus. He refused to use what He had for His own advantage.

What a confrontation with the often-selfish motives of our Christian life, its prayers and priorities.

"What is a Christian?" you may ask. The first answer is the easiest. A Christian is a believer in the sacrificial death and provision of Jesus Christ for his righteousness, believing in the total remission of sins and eternal relationship with the Father by faith.

But he is also one who has confessed Jesus as Lord (*kurios, despotes*). And, as Christ's servant, the believer acknowledges by legitimate, right-minded choice of mental disposition the place of self-emptying and self-crucifixion.

He accepts, as it were, "the spoiling of his goods" and the necessary "becoming of no reputation" so that the ultimate significance of Christ's glory and significance might be seen in him.

Please know this: It is not for nothing that the Scriptures record in Acts 11:26, "The disciples were first called Christians at *Antioch*."

Antioch was the slave capital of the Roman world in New Testament times! It was infamous for giving derogatory nicknames. History records the residents reportedly called the Emperor Julian "the Goat," and almost lost their lives!

"Christian" was a term of derision and mocking. It implied servility and obsequiousness. The Roman historian Tacitus wrote, "The *vulgar* call them Christians...," and W. E. Vine declares, "as applied by Gentiles, there was no doubt and implication of service."

Would You Pass for a Christian?

Someone once wrote, "If you were on trial for being a Christian, would there be enough evidence to convict you?" We might paraphrase, "Would any secular society surrounding you describe your existence by a term identifying you with self-renouncing service to Christ?"

A Christian is one "belonging to Christ," so the ending implies in the Greek. But "belonging to," as in ownership and servanthood — identified with the essence of conformity and likeness.

When the worldly society contemptuously called the early believers "Christians" — slaves of this Christ — the believers must have said, "That's the *nicest* thing anyone ever said about us!"

At least they began to use the term of derision as a title of almost sacred acceptance and self-definition. "I am a Christian, a servant/disciple of the Lord Jesus Christ. I am being conformed to His likeness, modeled in self-renunciation and humility and a life lived in ultimate obedience to the complete will of His Father. I am pleased to be known and identified with His image."

CHAPTER 3

Where Do Problems Come From?

I still want to know, "Why must a Christian have problems?" and, what's more, "Where do they come from?"

The Christian life is a process. It is never measured by the momentary, but by the *eternal*. It is going somewhere.

The dynamic of the Christian experience is that its measured progress is toward a specifically designed *goal*. There is no vague, sloppy, deceptive religious terminology to hide that truth.

The Christian is being conformed to the likeness of Christ's model as a willing servant/disciple of the Father. This is an obvious, discernable lifestyle, like marriage or a profession.

One doesn't arrive by pushing a button or endless imagining. It is attained by specific decisions and daily growth. The lifestyle is progressive and visible.

There is no single "experience" or Christian profession which brings such a likeness to pass, although growth and specific experiences of faith may speed the process and accelerate its attainment.

"What's All This About Push-Ups?"

Were you ever in the home of a young person who had tried out for an athletic team?

I remember when our son Chip went out for football. The process started when Chip went to the coach and said, "I'd like to be a football player."

Without even looking up, the coach said, "Do fifty push-ups."

When Chip had finished, the coach barked, "Run around the track three times."

After that, he directed, "Jog up and down the stadium seats four times."

I'm sure Chip must have been saying to himself, "I came to play football. What's all this about push-ups, running, and jogging?"

If you've experienced this yourself, or in a loved one's life, you remember what the following hours were like. The young man comes home, falls exhausted on his bed, and goes to sleep without dinner.

When he awakes the next morning, every bone in his body aches, and he walks to the shower like an eighty-year-old man! The young man's seemingly simple desire to play football has suddenly produced two problems in addition to simply matching him with an ultimate opponent.

Surprisingly, the coach himself has become an enemy, and the boy's body seems to find a voice and say to him, "Maybe *you* want to play football, turkey, but nobody asked *me!*"

Sources of the Christian's Problems

Surely you see the lesson. The Christian's problems have several sources, three of which are especially obvious.

First, there is a real adversary, Satan, who is the most diabolical problem of all. He is as his name implies: an accuser and slanderer committed to compromising our purpose with all the strategy, force, and skill of a life-long football opponent.

Second, there is also the struggle in our own flesh, our own human life, to oppose the necessary changes demanded by conformity to the image of Jesus Christ.

Third, surprisingly to some, the Holy Spirit Himself becomes a source of problems to believers when He takes on the role of "coach."

One young man wrote, "If, after an exhausting workout, the coach calls for five more laps or twenty more push-ups before hitting the showers, he represents a real problem! The flesh may rebel, but the spirit knows that the 'above and beyond' conditioning will give that small but important edge over the opponent."

In the following pages we will examine the three principal *sources* of the Christian's problems. However, one thing must be clear: *No problem comes to a believer unless it has been allowed by the Lord.*

"The Door of the Sheepfold"

Jesus Christ is the "door of the sheepfold." Specifically, He said, "Most assuredly, I say to you, I am the door of the sheep" (John 10:7).

The average sheep cote or fold was a small curb of rocks, or a fence which lacked a door or gate. When the shepherd had herded his flock inside, he simply lay down across the opening and became himself the door! Nothing or no one went out or came in except through him!

Certainly not everything that comes to a believer is either good or comes *from* the Lord. But the believer cannot be submerged in any experience unless the Lord has *permitted* the circumstances and intends a lesson and a victory out of it.

Job and his friends struggled with this, and so do we.

The Apostle Paul wrote:

No temptation has overtaken you except such as is common to man; but God is faithful, who will not allow you to be tempted beyond what you are able, *but with the temptation* will also make the way of escape, that you may be able to bear it"

1 Corinthians 10:13 (italics added)

21

The Ultimate Example

The context of this passage is the wilderness experience of Israel, which is to be an ultimate example of our learning experience:

> Now all these things happened to them as examples, and they were written for our admonition, on whom the ends of the ages have come.

> 1 Corinthians 10:11

"But wait a minute," someone will chime in. "I find somewhere in the Bible that God doesn't tempt *any* man. What about that?"

Often we are troubled by one word in our language which translates two separate ideas in the original language of the Scriptures. "Love" is an example. That one word covers at least four Greek words and concepts, ranging from eroticism all the way to sacrificial, unrequited, God-like *agape* love.

There *is* a passage that says:

> Let no one say when he is tempted, "I am tempted by God"; for God cannot be tempted by evil, nor does He Himself tempt anyone.

> But each one is tempted when he is drawn away by his own desires and enticed.

> James 1:13,14

"That's it!" you say. "I *knew* it was in there somewhere!"

Not so fast. This same chapter says:

> My brethren, count it all joy when you fall into various trials,

> knowing that the testing of your faith produces patience.

> James 1:2,3

And later:

> Blessed is the man who endures temptation; for when he has been proved, he will receive the crown of life which the Lord has promised to those who love Him.

> James 1:12

Tests, Trials, and Temptations

There *are* tests or trials — sometimes even translated "temptations" — which are connected to the concept of *proving*, generally connected with a form of the Greek, *dokimos*. However, this is in no way "temptation" to sin, for God has no part in sin.

Like the process of smelting or refining, this process is meant to bring forth the best and the purest, and to separate the impure and the useless.

In the latter process, God *does* take a part. The Levites said, "You are the Lord God, who chose Abram... You found his heart faithful before You..." (Nehemiah 9:7,9). Here the phrase "found faithful" is the strongest possible concept of testing and refinement. We will examine this Scripture more fully at a later time.

Perhaps we spend too much time asking where the problem originates. Of course, a part of the ultimate test may be standing in faith and believing over enemy opposition.

"Source" vs. "Purpose"

But perhaps the initial question before one of "source" should be one of "purpose." Why has this particular trial surfaced? What is it testing within me or my Christian experience in general?

Soon enough the Holy Spirit brings us enlightenment on what the source of the issue is and what we should do; however, our initial desire should be to understand the direction it is taking us.

Parents quickly discover how children learn to manipulate them. Our firstborn was a beautiful daughter who has always been somewhat "the apple of her father's eye."

She could crawl on my lap as a youngster, wrap her arms around my neck, look into my eyes and say, "I love you, Daddy," and my resistance melted. Soon, however, I got wise. My response became, "O.K., Cheri. What do you want now?"

Of course, her expressions were not insincere, nor were they always manipulatory. But too often the two emotions — expressing love and seeking or desiring something — became mixed or compromised.

True Worship Or a Personal Agenda?

So they are in us as we relate to our heavenly Father. Only the Holy Spirit can help us sort out the mixture of our true worship and our use of praise to push forth our own personal agenda.

One time when Cheri was a maturing adolescent, it was necessary for me to give a rather difficult discipline. She became very angry and responded, "I don't like you!" She ran to her room and slammed the door.

I was deeply hurt, but I knew that Cheri was simply overwhelmed by her personal disappointment. I stood in the living room, a bit stunned and also wanting to test my own spirit.

Soon I heard her bedroom door open, and she came to me with tears streaming down her face.

"Daddy," she said through her tears, "I don't hate you. I love you, and I know you're doing what you think is best for me. I still don't like it, and I disagree with your decision, but I love you and I accept what you've said."

Mature Love

When she put her arms around me, wetting my cheek with her tears, I knew she was expressing genuine, tested and proven love. It meant more to me than a hundred hurried "I love yous" when rushed into an expression of "Can I go here?" or "Can I have some money?" *This* was love from maturity; the love of trust even when an experience was distasteful or unpleasant.

Long after Cheri had quietly gone back to her bedroom, I stood alone with my own tears. I felt affirmed and comforted as a father. My daughter's love for me was more than a response to my provision for her, or the availability of my agreement or blessing. But my tears were also tears of conviction. How often had I spoken to my heavenly Father with such affirmation?

Prayer

We, as His children, should be able to respond to our heavenly Father with the following prayer:

"Father, I don't understand this experience. I don't like it. But I know You are a sovereign, caring, loving Father, and You only do or allow what is best for me. I love You for Yourself, not because You always please me or do what I want. Father, I love You. I love You as a mature, growing child who desires to always submit to your purpose."

CHAPTER 4

The Holy Spirit And Trouble

I have spoken frequently at conferences, some of which have been in the charismatic tradition. At one such conference, held in a world-famous charismatic center, I was asked to be a member of a panel made up of a Catholic priest, an Episcopal priest, a Presbyterian minister, and myself.

There was a question-and-answer session, which is not my favorite part of such a program. A contentious person pressed a doctrinal issue almost, I believe, in the hope of starting an argument among the panelists.

"And I want to ask Dr. ——," she said rather sarcastically, "just what is the evidence of the baptism of the Holy Spirit."

The Presbyterian beside me was the one on the spot, and I thought, "Oh, no, here it goes!" But without batting an eye, and with a smile of gracious understanding, my brother replied, "Lady, the evidence of the baptism in the Holy Spirit is..." and he paused dramatically, *"trouble!"* The crowd roared its approval. I turned to him and said, "Right on!"

Increasing Our Maturity

Each experience in the Holy Spirit is meant to increase the level of our maturity. After Jesus' baptism, the Scriptures record:

And immediately the Spirit drove Him into the wilderness.

27

And He was there in the wilderness forty days, tempted by Satan, and was with the wild beasts; and the angels ministered to Him.

Mark 1:12,13

The Greek word translated "drove" in Mark 1 is *ekballo*, and is related to the very ending of the word pro*blem*. It means "to cast out, send, or thrust forth."

There is much light on the Holy Spirit's leadership which comes from a study of Mark's account. Christ went in the propelling force and energy of the Spirit. But — let us not miss this — He was sent by the Spirit to face Satan, and was empowered by the Holy Spirit for the battle to be waged in the wilderness.

Led by the Spirit into the wilderness, Christ was taken to physical hunger, and that hunger was a process in the economy of God. It was a condition in the will of God. *Jesus was hungry because He was in God's will.*

When Satan first attacked Christ, it was on the issue of the will of the Father for Him, and Christ answered from Deuteronomy 8:3:

So He humbled you, allowed you to hunger, and fed you with manna which you did not know nor did your fathers know, that He might make you know that man shall not live by bread alone; but man lives by every word that proceeds from the mouth of the Lord.

Was Jesus misquoting Scripture to justify His hunger and test? Deuteronomy 8:5 continues what indeed must have been in our Lord's mind when He answered Satan:

So you should know in your heart that as a man chastens his son, so the Lord your God chastens you.

The Mark of Sonship

My friend on the panel was indeed accurate: The mark of the Spirit's anointing and leadership — indeed the mark of sonship — is the testing and chastening work of the Holy Spirit. He, as a divine *coach*, accepts the responsibility to arrange the circumstances which will promote our maturity and bring us into the likeness of a servant; the mental disposition and positive discipline of our Lord Jesus Christ.

And for our flesh and the enemies of Christian maturity, that action of the Holy Spirit spells t-r-o-u-b-l-e.

On the positive side, those experiences are the arenas in which we are being changed from glory (or significance) to glory into the same likeness: the likeness of the Lord Jesus Christ (2 Corinthians 3:18).

The Hebrew word for "glory" is especially plain. *Kabod* is a word that means "weight" or "significance." Believers should not envision some flimsy, cloud nine, ethereal presence. *The glory of the Lord is the weight and significance of His purpose circumscribed on our earthly lives.* The Greek word for "likeness" itself, *eikon*, is the specific concept of sculpturing or transforming.

Do you remember our illustration of the young man who volunteered for the football team? He did not envision what would have to take place between his "signing up" and the moment he would take his place on the field with his teammates. Our young friend could only envision screaming fans and the success of a triumphant run or good block against a competing high school team.

The Coach's Perspective

His coach saw the young man from an entirely different perspective! He saw the necessity of muscles being tightened and endurance being tested to the limit in order to increase capacity. He knew that the young man needed grueling daily exposure to tests of blocking, running, tackling, and enduring.

When the coach takes our young man and his colleagues through endless push-ups, running, tackling exercises, blocking practices, and play-learning sessions, it is not arbitrary or unnecessary.

To put the boy in a game without such practice and preparation would be disastrous. The same holds true for basic military training. Young men hate their drill instructors in basic training and love them in the heat of battle. Sending untrained men into battle is murder.

When the Levites in the passage from Nehemiah 9 described God's action in Abraham's life, they described seven actions on God's part. Can you find them in this Scripture?

> **You are the Lord God, who chose Abram, and brought him out of Ur of the Chaldees, and gave him the name Abraham;**
>
> **You found his heart faithful before You, and made a covenant with him to give the land of the Canaanites, the Hittites, the Amorites, the Perizzites, the Jebusites, and the Girgashites — to give it to his descendants. You have performed Your words, for You are righteous.**

Nehemiah 9:7,8

God chose Abram in Genesis 12 and brought him out of Ur, but He didn't change his name or confirm the covenant until Genesis 17. Why not confirm the covenant in the time of the call? Because, the Scripture answers, God had to find Abram's heart to be faithful to Himself.

Finding Out by Inquiry

Here is a difficult but imperative truth. The word in the Septuagint, or Greek Old Testament, used heavily in Jesus' time, is *eurisko*. It means "to find out by inquiry, to learn or to discern." The Hebrew word in the same Scripture is *matsa*, which, as we have seen, is a word of refining or smelting and means "to cause something to come forth."

How often have we said of someone going through a crisis, "That seemed to bring the very best out of him"? Or, in disappointment, we will say, "That seemed to bring out the very worst in him."

Does God need to discover something about us? Apparently. And, we must hurriedly note, it has nothing to do with our justification or our salvation.

The question before us is whether or not we can be brought into our purpose; into the design and dream of God for our lives.

Abraham Believed God

Abram faced five clear tests in Genesis 12 through 17, none of which concerned his justification. The Scripture is clear on that point: "And he believed in the Lord, and He accounted it to him for righteousness" (Genesis 15:6); and "Abraham believed God, and it was accounted to him for righteousness" (Romans 4:3).

Salvation, says Paul, "is of faith that it might be according to grace" (Romans 4:16). It is "the righteousness of God which is through faith in Jesus Christ to all and on all who believe" (Romans 3:22). Such believers are "justified freely by His grace through the redemption that is in Christ Jesus" (Romans 3:24).

What, then, is God discovering in us through tests? If it has nothing to do with salvation, what, then, is the purpose of the trial? The answer is devastatingly simple and intricately difficult at the same time.

For Abraham, it was whether or not he could come into God's ultimate purpose of blessing and usefulness. Lucifer didn't pass his test. The generations up to Noah didn't. One could argue that Noah himself didn't. Although he came through deliverance, he seemed to miss the order of a restored world; at least those who followed him missed it.

For you and me, the issue is God's vision for our lives: fulfilled servanthood, released anointing, and consummate ministry.

Abraham's Five Tests

Abram faced five unique and specific tests before the covenant was confirmed. Incidently, during that same period of time (Genesis 12-17), he also had five appearances of God (Genesis 12:1-3; 12:7; 13:14-18; 15:5, and 17:1-21).

It would be sheer folly to argue concerning the sources of the tests. One was brought through natural drought or famine; one through an unbelieving but generous king; another through a carnal nephew; and the fourth through a doubting wife.

Who cares what container the test arrives in? In each circumstance, God was looking for a specific quality of faith in Abraham, such as: fervor, sufficiency, humility, integrity, and

Trial No.	Scripture	Test Description	Context Of the Test	Issues at Stake	*Qualities* of Faith Being Tested
1.	Gen. 11,12	Willingness to break the ties of nature. (Leave home and kindred.)	Ur	Separation	*Fervor of faith*
2.	Gen. 12: 10-20	Stress of circumstances (Famine in Canaan.)	Egypt	Famine	*Sufficiency of faith*
3.	Gen.13: 1-18	Unity vs. friction with Lot.	Strife	Riches	*Humility*
4.	Gen. 14	Love for brethren and dependance on God.	Kings of North and Sodom	Power	*Integrity*
5.	Gen. 16	Time of waiting for birth of son.	His wife Sarai	Delay	*Patience*

patient truth.

The simple chart helps you see the issues at stake and the nature of the test itself. Review the chart briefly before going on with our text.

"How did Abram do?" you might ask.

"How would you do?" I might counter. Aren't the issues vaguely familiar to you: natural ties, circumstantial stress, friction among brethren, the integrity of personal freedom, and the overwhelming difficulty of delay. (See chart, above.)

I can't be overly objective with these issues, because their personal implications are too painful. Notice, too, that some of the tests occurred during the seeming silence of God. Thirteen years probably elapsed between the last two tests, and twenty-five years were between Abram's original call and the covenant confirmation.

That's where it's tough — holding to a word of promise when there are plenty of tests, but God doesn't seem to be talking!

Joseph's Tests

The Psalmist said, concerning Joseph, "Until the time that his word came to pass, the word of the Lord tested him" (Psalm 105:19).

What tests did Joseph experience? He was sold as a slave; they hurt his feet with fetters; and "he was laid in irons." Some scholars argue that the last phrase is better translated, "the fetters passed into his spirit or soul."

We understand that, don't we? It's one thing to be given a charismatic dream of usefulness and importance as a sixteen-year-old boy. It's quite another thing to let that vision test you throughout a lifetime until it comes to pass.

It often isn't the devil or this world that tests us; it's the Word itself which tests us. It's the harrowing time between promise and fulfillment; between vision and reality. Oh, to be faithful in *that* time!

Passing the Test

"How did Abraham do?"

What score is registered beside the grade sheet of Abram? The answer is as mixed and different as the question. He passed, obviously. His name was changed, and the covenant was confirmed.

Abraham is the father of all who believe and the progenitor of all who are justified by faith. God's commencement speech over Abraham is that he "obeyed," "went out," "sojourned," "waited," "was tested," and considered "God was able" — all of which he did through faith (Hebrews 11:8-19).

But God not only gives you the final grade; He shows you the work sheets. They reveal humanity, indecision, fear, running, nightmares, sinful presumption, carnal and fleshly activity. The same Scripture that tells us "he had received the promises" tells us he "heeded or leaned upon the voice of Sarai" and conceived a child out of the purposes of God.

Perhaps we should note that in Abram's tests we learn an important principle of God's grading system. The severe famine in Canaan, shortly after Abram's arrival, was a marvelous opportunity to prove the sufficiency and faithfulness of God.

Instead, Abram fled to Egypt, even passing off Sarai, his wife, to Pharaoh as his sister! Who would want such a man for a son-in-law?

Returning to Bethel

It took plagues and revelation upon an ungodly leader to turn Abram's entourage back toward Bethel, the place of spiritual beginnings. Genesis 13:3 says, "And he went on his journey," which could as easily be read, "He returned by his stations or campfires."

Abram, and any other believer being conformed to God's purpose, must return to the correct direction for their life by revisiting their steps into the failure.

Spiritually, we call this return journey repentance and restitution. The forgiveness of sins, already provided for in the once-sufficient death and resurrection of Jesus Christ, must be appropriated. Believers must "confess" or agree with God as to the nature of the failure. Biblically, we must pay back what we owe.

But never forget the end. When Abram returned to Bethel and rebuilt the altar, we see in verse 4 the first example of worship — "And there Abram called on the name of the

Lord" — and within ten verses, God gives Abram the greatest promise yet!

Until then, God had promised to show Abram the land. Now He promises to give him all the land — northward, southward, eastward, and westward (verse 14).

Victory Out of Failure

How unlike God we are. Here is the heavenly Grader granting the greatest promise to Abram following what we would consider his greatest failure! But *the issue is how you see the test!* God views the process in its entirety. Yes, Abram failed entirely and miserably. But he also learned, turned, returned, and worshipped — and God gives him an A+ for the process.

What a promise to us! What a hope for our tests! It *is* the process, not the momentary product of our test, which merits the Father's careful scrutiny.

"I see that you've learned," He says to us.

"But I've failed so miserably," we cry.

"Oh, yes, I know that," He speaks reassuringly. "I've seen the failure — but look how you responded. You're different. You've matured. You've learned. I'm pleased!"

CHAPTER 5

We Have Met The Enemy and It Is Us!

There were two decisive days that occurred in connection with the liberation of Europe during World War II.

The first was June 6, 1944, called D Day, the great day of the Normandy Invasion, with its landing of multiplied thousands of Allied troops in France.

The second, May 8, 1945, at the end of the conflict, was simply called V-E Day, for Victory Over Europe.

D Day marked a critical landing; a marvelous but costly "beginning of the end" of the conflict. However, many battles and much sacrifice took place before the ultimate victory was realized. In other words, it is a long way from the raising of a flag and the claiming of a territory to ultimate surrender and total conquest.

The Believer's D Day

The believer's D Day is when, by faith, he confesses Jesus Christ as Lord and Savior. God sends forth His Spirit into our life, and "The Spirit Himself bears witness with our spirit that we are children of God" (Romans 8:16).

But that wonderful day only *begins* the process of reclaiming our total life, its energies and potential, for the kingdom of God. It is as though the Spirit of God raises the flag on the beachhead of our life, like a group of Marines landing on the beachheads of the South Pacific.

"I claim this total life for God!" He proclaims. "I pronounce this person a child of God and joint-heir with the Son, Jesus Christ!"

That's when the "fun" begins, for the opposition is deeply planted in bunkers, on hilltops, in foxholes, and behind emplacements.

"You can claim what you want," a demonic voice seems to say, "but getting possession is another matter. Just try to displace me!"

The Marines move forward inch by inch. To go too quickly would allow the enemy to cut off the supply lines. Every territory has to be secured. This battle is for real, and the stakes are high.

Instant Salvation?

Many people expect an experience of New Birth and justification to bring instant salvation and quick maturity. A study of verb tenses in the New Testament Greek is always reassuring in this regard.

There is a past and finished salvation, called *justification*, which allows a believer to boldly confess, "I *was* saved. The penalty for my sin has been cancelled, and I am a new creation in Christ Jesus."

However, there is an equal case for cautiously saying, "I am *being* saved." This is the progressive sense or *sanctification*, in which the Holy Spirit is surely and certainly dealing with the power of sin in the believer's life.

Bill Gothard, the fine teacher of Christian principles, has encouraged Christians to wear buttons with the letters PBPGINFWMY boldly stamped on them. No, it's not a foreign language. It stands for "Please be patient. God is not finished with me yet."

Of course, there is also a clear biblical case for the future verb tense in salvation. It is right to earnestly confess, "I shall *be* saved" — and that's not wishful thinking!

God's Down Payment on Us

Paul calls the Holy Spirit's current witness and activity in the believer's experience an "earnest" — or a down payment — and a first fruit. He also says clearly that our salvation is in hope; furthermore:

> ...hope that is seen is not hope; for why does one still hope for what he sees?
>
> But if we hope for what we do not see, then we eagerly wait for it with perseverance.

> **Romans 8:24,25**

D Day in Christ is the firm confidence that there will be a true V-E Day. In the meantime, there is a sense of incompleteness and the continuation of a struggle.

Paul, in Romans 8, shows the creation, ourselves, and even the Holy Spirit *groaning* toward a moment of full completion. There is not doubt about its fulfillment, for:

> He who did not spare His own Son, but delivered Him up for us all, how shall He not with Him also freely give us all things?

> **Romans 8:32**

There can be no charges, no condemnation, and ultimately no separation for the believer. We are, by full comprehension, fully victors. But we are also "eagerly waiting for the adoption, the redemption of our body" (Romans 8:23).

"I don't like that," you say. "I want to get it over with quickly!"

Let's Kill the Devil

I am reminded of a small boy who asked, "Mommy, why doesn't God kill the devil and get it all settled?" Does his argument make sense, or doesn't it? Even a cursory reading of Judges 2:20-3:4 might help us.

Why did God leave some of the enemy in Canaan?

"Because His people didn't drive out the Canaanites completely, as they were instructed to," you respond.

Partially right, according to Scripture. Some of the enemy remained because the children of Israel transgressed the covenant, but also so the Lord might do the following:

...test Israel, whether they will keep the ways of the Lord....

...that the generations of the children of Israel might be taught to know war, at least those who had not formerly known it.

And they were left, that He might test Israel by them, to know whether they would obey the commandments of the Lord....

Judges 2:22; 3:2,4

God's Payday

God's payday doesn't always fall on Friday. God doesn't always grade us on immediate experience, but on continuing progress. Finals aren't taken the first week of class. The game isn't over in the first inning; nor is a war won by a single first strike.

The race is not always to the swift, as the ancient fable, "The Tortoise and the Hare," sought to prove to us. The Christian experience is *a race* — *agona* in the original Greek — an endurance of pressing.

We are to run with patience, courageous fortitude, pressing toward the mark for the prize of the high or approved calling in Christ Jesus. There is no time for us to indulge in self-satisfied back-patting. It's time to get on with the process of change!

An Interior Dog Fight

"How is it with you now that you're saved?" a cocky young seminarian asked a recently converted American Indian chief.

"Oh, well," he replied, "now it's like two great dogs are fighting inside of me."

Perplexed by the answer, and with more head knowledge than heart reality, the student pushed the issue.

"How can that be?" he asked.

"One is a great black dog," the chief answered, almost amused. "That's the old Indian chief. And one is a great white dog, the Great Holy Spirit."

Casually, the young man said, "O.K. — but which one wins?"

That was exactly the question the chief wanted. "Whichever one I feed the most," he retorted, rubbing his chin.

Feed Your New Nature

Over the centuries of Church history, various revivals and subsequent groups have urged an experience that would forever end this quandary, and rightfully so.

The Christian is not meant to live a powerless and defeated life. There is a decisive, victorious overcoming potential available to believers. But to teach that the conflict can be ultimately and completely settled short of biblical adoption (the placing of sons before the Father, the ultimate Redemption of the body) is unscriptural and sooner or later disillusioning.

If a believer continues to feed his "new nature" in Christ Jesus through obedience, discipline, prayer, and the Word of God, that nature becomes gigantic.

Starve Your Old Nature

On the other hand, the starving of the old nature through denial of lusts and fantasies, the refusal of material priorities, and the squelching of the flesh leaves it weakened, powerless, and all but dead.

But reverse the process, even for a day, and the old nature comes alive and pounds the new nature up against the wall. "Think me dead?" it seems to taunt us. "I revive quickly."

The second major source of the Christian's problems is the struggle in the believer's own life — his body and nature —

against the necessary changes and disciplines which will bring him to the image and likeness of Jesus Christ.

I have already confessed that my midlife crisis was long and severe. It was mainly spiritual, but there were the physical symptoms as well. I became acutely aware of the "B Day Complex": baldness, bifocals, bridges, bulges, and bunions!

In the process, my wife, Anita, arranged a membership in a prominent health studio for me. She picked out a beautiful, color-coordinated set of shorts, socks, shirts, and shoes for me. Even the gym bag matched. Then she patted me on the fanny and said, basically, "Go work out, buddy!"

I am convinced that they pick the biggest, ugliest people available to run those places. I think it's a conspiracy to threaten people like me. I arrived at the door of the men's workout room to find such a specter staring down at me. (I've never believed in Darwinian evolution, but I noted the similarities.)

"And what can I do for you?" he asked in a rumbling voice, staring at my color-coordinated outfit and bright tennies.

"I have a new membership," I said, my voice breaking like a teenager's. "I — I just want to get started in a program."

What he said next was such an insult that I'd have kicked him in the shins if I could have reached them.

"And what do you hope to accomplish?" he asked satirically, a smirk on his face.

I wanted to say something like, "Oh, I just want to be Mr. America in ten days," but instead I mumbled something about redistributing weight, and he beckoned me inside.

Medieval Man's Descendants Discovered

Now, I am basically a historian, and that day in the mirror-covered walls of that studio, I made a historic discovery. I found nearly all the direct descendants of medieval torture chambers! They couldn't fool *me* with their shining chrome and leather!

The specter gleefully took me to each piece, requiring some mandatory obeisance at each place. Finally we were at the *piece de resistance*, which he had purposely saved until last.

"Lie down on this bench," he commanded, adjusting the weights on a sliding bar.

"Now push this up ten times!" I felt like I was back in gym class with the mean Italian drill sergeant of my youth.

Mostly in sheer frustration, I pushed the bar up five times. The sixth and seventh times were harder, the eighth difficult, the ninth impossible. Out of sheer anger at his lurking presence, I finally gathered the strength for the final tenth push. I heard the bar lock in place, and I breathed deeply.

With fingers outstretched, shadowing my face like a weapon, he shouted, "FIVE MORE!"

"You're crazy," I said.

"FIVE MORE!" he repeated louder.

I felt now like the entire studio was watching. "But I can't. It hurts," I finally whimpered.

"The Theology of Health"

That's what he was waiting for. Lights flashed, music played in the background, and I heard for the first time "the theology of health" thundered from the Mount Sinai of all such places.

"NO PAIN," he almost yelled, "NO GAIN!"

I will never reveal what I said on that occasion, justified by the incompleteness of my sanctification. But my subsequent visits were much quieter and more private.

But dislike it or not, it's a fact of life: "Growing pains" are not metaphoric. They are real and spiritual recognitions of change and development. Indeed, we have met the enemy, and it is ourselves!

I am a mixture, and so are you. A little bit of heaven and a whole lot of earth combine in my person. I am in love with God and pursuing holiness, but I'm all too alive in a body which is not yet redeemed. And the answer is not wishing away the conflict or searching for an experience to end it all.

There is growth in the process. Change is the act of becoming — not always in being. That's the dynamic of the Christian life — being metamorphosized; being conformed and changed. Our metamorphosis is seldom compressed into an instant, or even into a specific experience.

There are victories and there are great moments of faith and will when we surrender to the Holy Spirit vast areas of previously carnal life. But even with these, the overall victory is gradual, progressive, and much more a process than an experience.

A Dangerous Battle

However, the danger of this battle is almost overwhelming. The flesh wars against the spirit, for they are indeed contrary to one another. In one of the strongest passages of Scripture in the Bible, the Apostle Paul describes his own conflict:

Therefore I run thus: not with uncertainty. Thus I fight: not as one who beats the air.

But I discipline my body and bring it into subjection, lest, when I have preached to others, I myself should become disqualified.

1 Corinthians 9:26,27

Like the famous passage in Romans 7, the great apostle is here acknowledging the ever-present danger of indwelling weakness to prevent God's purpose in his life. Here his terms are of the utmost in spiritual athletics.

First Corinthians 9 in general is a transparent defense of the apostolic office and Paul's unclaimed privileges and rights. It is a typical mixed list of freedoms available through Christ, but restricted by choice. Scholars often call attention to the passage because of its strong athletic imagery.

Notice, Paul states that the believer is neither running without fixed and certain goals, nor is he shadowboxing or feinting to make his blows tell.

Christian victory and warfare are not for cream puffs. And the principal enemy we fight is not the devil! It is our flesh — the predisposition within our unredeemed body with our human nature — to demand ease and avoid discipline.

"Benched by the Coach"

And what is the greatest danger to us? It is the horrendous potential in verse 27 that by yielding to our flesh we become "disqualified" — *adokimos* — rejected as unusable and benched by the coach at the most strategic moment of the contest.

Mercifully, there is not the slightest suggestion of our being cast away from faith in this passage. Instead, the danger is the awful potential of failing to achieve our specific purpose.

This passage in First Corinthians 9 does not speak of some agonizing uncertainty in attempting to win eternal life. Rather, it provides the pattern of responsible discipline in the fulfillment of Christian purpose and ministry.

How can we avoid the disappointment and embarrassment of missed direction and waylaid purpose? The apostle here uses two verbs concerning his action upon his own body which imply the utmost in rigorous, almost sadistic control in order that the body might serve and not hinder his progress toward the goal of Christian victory and ultimate reward.

"I *discipline* my body," one translation renders verse 27. Actually, in the original Greek, it is a strong word for "striking under the eye or beating black and blue."

How Paul Battled His Greatest Enemy

One could easily paraphrase verse 27, "I turn the boxing gloves upon my own body, and I *beat* my flesh black and blue!" Paul is here determined that his body must *never* become the enemy of his spiritual purpose. Therefore, he denies it; he buffets it!

In verse 27, the apostle says that he works on the body to "bring it into subjection." Here again, the real strength of the original language is almost untranslatable. It basically means "to lead into slavery, or to make or treat as a slave."

Reader, you must grasp this intensity! Paul is saying, "My flesh — the warfare in my nature — is a source of unlimited problems to me."

Standing before the Lord Jesus Christ at His *bema* judgment, every believer will receive "the things done in the body, according to what he has done, whether good or bad" (2 Corinthians 5:10).

This is not the reward seat of a modern Olympic game, but the reward seat of the Lord Himself! To understand this requires very specific discipline and choice during these days of our walk on earth. No wonder in a parallel passage concerning the Christian race and discipline, the Word admonishes:

> **Therefore, since we are receiving a kingdom which cannot be shaken, let us have grace, by which we may serve God acceptably with reverence and godly fear.**
>
> **For our God is a consuming fire.**
>
> **Hebrews 12:28,29**

CHAPTER 6

The Devil Made Me Do It

An amusing story concerns a believer who discovered the devil sitting on the curb in front of a local church. The devil is weeping profusely because he is being blamed for so much happening inside the church that he had nothing to do with!

Haven't you found that blaming it on the devil — "The devil made me do it" — is often an excuse for not being honest and taking responsibility for our failures? I certainly have.

Nevertheless, Satan is a powerful and dangerous adversary who knows our weaknesses and flaws. Furthermore, he is armed with a powerful arsenal, and he knows how to use it to his advantage to sidetrack the believer from meaningful discipleship and personal purpose.

Truly, we must be freed from the mythological and comical figure of Satan as having horns, tail, and pitchfork. Satan is a created being who is not omnipresent, omnipotent, or omniscient. He does, however, control a world system of principalities, powers, rulers of the darkness of this age, and spiritual hosts of wickedness, according to Ephesians 6:12.

In her excellent devotional on Ephesians, *Life on the Highest Plane*, published by Baker Book House, Ruth Paxson says that Satan attempts the following three things in the believer's life:

1. To *despoil* the Christian of his wealth
2. To *decoy* the Christian from his walk

3. To *disable* the Christian from his warfare

What a strategy! How often the enemy wins in the believer's life without even firing a shot!

The Third Source of Problems

Later we shall look at the entire arena of the chief enemy's warfare against believers. Now, however, we simply want to address *Satan's presence and strategy as a third source of the Christian's problems.*

We must always hold this subject in balance, realizing that Satan has been defeated and stripped of actual authority by the cross of Jesus Christ.

Through His sacrificial death, Christ "...disarmed principalities and powers, He made a public spectacle of them, triumphing over them in it" (Colossians 2:14).

Yet, Paul warns "lest Satan should take advantage of us; for we are not ignorant of his devices" (2 Corinthians 2:11); and Peter advises:

> Be sober, be vigilant; because your adversary the devil walks about like a roaring lion, seeking whom he may devour.
>
> Resist him, steadfast in the faith, knowing that the same sufferings are experienced by your brotherhood in the world.
>
> **1 Peter 5:8,9**

Satan and his forces, like the old nature of the flesh itself, have been crushed and mortally wounded by Christ's faithful, obedient act of servanthood and suffering. But to think of Satan as a toothless and powerless foe is both dangerous and unscriptural.

Like the kingdom of God itself, which is "already" and "not yet," so Satan is both cast down and still has access; he is both totally defeated but is living out final moments of residency in this earth. His notice has been given, and we need not live in fear of him, but he continues to live out a spiritual authority which makes him an influential opponent to our Christian purpose.

A Unique Conversation About Satan

There is a unique and revealing conversation between Jesus and Peter on the night of Jesus' betrayal and trial. Calling him by a little boy's name — a reminder of his past — the Lord said, "Simon, Simon! Indeed, Satan has asked for you, that he may sift you as wheat" (Luke 22:31).

The word "asked for" in this passage is actually a much stronger word which generally means "to demand" for trial, or "to require something due."

A consistent and perhaps bolder translation would be, "Simon, Satan has demanded you for trial, that he might hold possession of your ability — riddling and sifting your faith."

"Can he do that?" you ask.

Apparently. Satan, or Lucifer, was the angel who covered; the defender of God's authority. There is the scriptural place of his appearance before God's throne in accusation and the ability to try or test.

Jesus continued in this passage from Luke by saying to Peter, "But I have prayed for you, that your faith should not fail; and when you have returned to Me, strengthen your brethren" (Luke 22:32).

Again, it is important to see that Peter's returning might as easily be translated, "when you have *been* twisted or turned about," and relates directly to the word "strengthen your brethren."

It could be argued that Jesus was warning Peter that the experience would be like a vortex, involving much twisting about for his life and faith. Jesus' prayer was that Peter's faith would not "utterly fail" in the experience.

It was an experience, as we can see from hindsight through the Scriptures, which would test Peter's courage, his identity with Jesus, and his truthfulness and integrity. Ultimately, it would bring him into open despair, guilt, and feelings of worthlessness.

Why Did Peter Turn?

Why Peter? The disciples were all tested. They all, in effect, forsook our Lord and fled into the night. Perhaps it could be argued that Peter's greater confession — "Lord, I am ready..." (Luke 22:33), or "Even if all are made to stumble because of You, I will never be made to stumble" (Matthew 26:33) — set him up for a greater fall.

I am persuaded, however, that the reason for the greater and more obvious trial is found in the nature of Peter's greater and more obvious calling and purpose. It is a principle in all of life that the greater the projected release, authority, or purpose, the greater the trial, test, and pressure. The results are almost proportional.

The larger the ministry, the more exciting the destiny, the greater and more challenging the preparation required and the testing demanded. Peter was to be a leader. His personal vortex would prepare him to help his brothers in this twisting arena.

Satan in the Old Testament

There is an interesting and revealing Old Testament picture of Satan's devices in the third chapter of the prophecy of Zechariah. Here, in the fourth of eight visions young Zechariah received in just one January night, he sees his contemporary High Priest, Joshua, in deep trouble.

Joshua is seen standing before the Lord, and Satan is standing at his right hand to oppose him. Joshua and his sidekick Zerubbabel had been assigned the great task of bringing back from Babylonian captivity the first fruits of restoration: about 50,000 tattered and unimportant captives compared with those who stayed in Babylon.

They had a great task, assigned from God through the contemporary superpower, Cyrus. Their task was to reconstruct the Temple of God in Jerusalem. And although some help came from Cyrus and their still-in-Babylon relatives, the returnees' task seemed basically overwhelming.

Then, as they started digging about in the blackened circle of earth that had been Jerusalem, they faced the opposition of neighbors using force and political intrigue, as well as the wearying discouragement of weeping colleagues who compared the new work with older grandeur.

Devastating Discouragement

The results were devastating. Shortly after beginning to build, they surrendered the task in defeat, and for sixteen long years the unfinished Temple was a mocking charade to the purposes of God.

How typical of the calls to restoration we have had in our lives: Rebuild the family altar, repay broken vows, and restore our disrupted stewardship.

Scripture reveals the reasons for the failures: Samaritans, political letters, lack of resources. But Zechariah's vision concerning leadership is more accurate and, from God's viewpoint, more spiritually revealing: *Satan stood up to oppose them!*

The young High Priest, Joshua, born himself in captivity to Judah's last spiritual leader, had never even seen the Temple! In the rush of the discouraging and overwhelming assignment, he had made a tragic decision.

He permitted the younger refugees to intermarry with peoples of the land, probably thinking to strengthen their population and perhaps produce peace with the neighbors. As always, sin multiplied itself.

This wrong decision, and the intermarriages themselves, were to haunt the restoration for its remaining days until the situation was finally resolved under the legal reform of the priest-prophet Ezra.

Joshua's Failure and Sin

"Now Joshua was clothed with filthy garments, and was standing before the Angel," Zechariah records of his vision (Zechariah 3:3). Hebrew scholars tell us that the word "filthy" is actually excrement bespattered, obscene, smelly, and beyond description.

The failure and sin both of Joshua personally and, as he stood in his representational ministry for all the people, was very real — startlingly real.

Satan is obviously legalistic in his accusation, probably quoting whole chapters of Leviticus: "How dare you come before the Lord in such a filthy condition?"

Zechariah hears the Lord say to Satan, "The Lord rebuke you, Satan! Is this not a brand plucked from the fire?" (verse 2).

One hardly needs comment on this truth. "I understand the nature of his weakness," the Lord seems to reply. "He came out of the fire. I knew him totally when I chose him. I rebuke and perpetually rebuke you, Satan."

What follows is such a swift action that Zechariah must have thought his vision was being fastforwarded! The filthy garments are ordered removed, and "rich robes" are provided.

During it all, Zechariah becomes so excited that he jumps into his own vision! (Don't ask me how you do that.) "And I said, 'Let them put a clean turban on his head.' So they put a clean turban on his head, and they put the clothes on him..." Zechariah records (verse 5).

Surely you see the deeper understanding of this passage. Here Joshua, under attack by Satan, yields to a spirit of guilt and condemnation which debilitates him. His failure represents sixteen long years of inaction and incomplete work for God.

This failure was brought to pass not so much by sin — which could, and obviously was, immediately forgiven — but by sixteen long years of accusation and immobilization.

Joshua faced sixteen long years of spiritual attack through the clever devices of an archenemy. What a revealing picture this is — what a commentary on so many believers and so much of the work of God.

"A Zechariah 3 Moment"

I remember a key moment in my own personal pilgrimage. There was seeming defeat in my ministry and my marriage. My wife encouraged me to find someone to fill my pulpit and to go away alone to a favorite retreat on the ocean near San Diego. It was "a Zechariah 3 moment" in my life, although I was not making the spiritual connection.

Condemnation, guilt, and horrendous feelings of inadequacy and failure dogged my every moment. I didn't even take a Bible on the trip. But, as usual, those Gideons will get you every time!

I stumbled into my cottage late one Saturday night and awoke the next morning to find a Gideon Bible on the coffee table. More out of habit than desire, I picked up the Bible, and it opened to Zechariah 3! Only this time, I gave it neither historic nor expositional attention: I saw *myself* in the situation.

I felt the disabling effect of condemnation; the paralysis of accusation. It was *my* dirty garments, and Satan's attack upon *my* life and purpose. Hot tears flowed down my cheeks as I finished the chapter. I felt anger and resentment in my spirit.

"Tell me, God," I almost yelled at the ceiling, "why did You wait sixteen years to tell him he was forgiven and accepted in spite of his failure? Huh? How come sixteen years?" Anger boiled in me. It was an expression of my own hurt and frustration.

If ever God's Spirit spoke to me, it was in that moment. Sweetly, with patience and understanding, He seemed to say, "I didn't wait sixteen years to *tell* him, son. He waited sixteen years to *hear!*"

CHAPTER 7

Arenas and Victors:
The Spiritual Olympiad

I once visited Munich, Germany, the scene of the ill-fated 1972 World Olympiad events.

The Olympic stadium is magnificent, engineered with a precise German sense of function and the perfect balance of greenbelts and parks, waterways and fountains, along with actual performance stadiums.

There is one area, or *platz*, which has three levels of silver plaques commemorating the bronze, silver, and gold medal winners in that unique and heralded athletic competition.

But for all its planning and expensive construction, the *Olympiazentrum* of Munich is far less than it was in the crowning moment of excitement as participants and spectators from many nations crowded the tracks and halls, and jammed the seating capacity of each arena.

Specific Arenas of Conflict

Believers also face their problems, struggles, and contests in *specific arenas*. These arenas are not designed by prize-winning contemporary architects, but by the agents of purpose and conflict in the Christian experience.

These spiritual arenas are not built of concrete, steel, and glass, but of the elements of human nature and spiritual warfare. Nevertheless, these arenas of the Christian's problems are real, and their contests are authentic.

The Apostle Paul frequently interposed the believer's struggle upon the model of his contemporary Olympiad, called the Isthmian games. He must have often been there; the language of athletic discipline, contest, and reward appears everywhere in his writings.

Three Ravaging Forces

Basically, the Scriptures reveal that the believer faces his conflicts in three specific arenas: (1) the world, (2) the flesh, and (3) the devil. Ephesians 2:1-3 gives us a glance at these three, calling them, "the course of this world," "the prince of the power of the air, the spirit who now works in the sons of disobedience," and "the lusts of our flesh."

These are the three ravaging forces which form the whole lifestyle of "the children of wrath," which included all of us before we were made alive with Christ and saved by His grace!

As we shall see, the Bible gives us unique, specific descriptions of these arenas and reveals the points at which they operate in all our lives.

Spiritual Alternatives

Contrary to each of the opposition forces, there are specific spiritual *alternatives* in each of the three arenas. The world system, for example, is biblically counterbalanced through the revealed Word of God and the specific will of the Father.

Since, as we will later see in detail, the world system is basically a system of ideas and slogans which form materialistic life patterns, *the real struggle between the world and the Word of God is in the mind of mankind.* In a sense, the mind is the battleground for this first and preeminently foundational arena of the Christian and his or her problems.

The flesh, or *man's sensual nature apart from God, is clearly opposed by the Spirit of God.* Indeed, "the flesh lusts against the Spirit, and the Spirit against the flesh; and these are contrary to one another, so that you do not do the things that you wish" (Galatians 5:17).

The flesh targets two specific areas of man which therefore become the battleground of this arena. These targets are *the human body* and *the human spirit.*

Again, as in an athletic contest, the two opposing forces seem to compete for control in these areas, and the conflict itself becomes a major contribution to the believer's problems.

Third, each believer faces an arena of conflict which, for want of a better designation, we will simply call "the devil." Satan is not only a source of our problems; his specific attacks against our purpose become an entire arena of our conflict.

Here the attack is against our destiny and the divine or ultimate intention for our lives. This is an arena in which *the enemy attempts to immobilize the believer from the realization of "the dream" of God in his life — the ultimate purpose God has planned for the believer.*

The goal in this conflict is either the debilitation or the release of the believer into fulfillment and purpose. In many ways, the battle in this arena is the most acute, and its ramifications last the longest and are the farthest reaching.

Three Special Heroes

One can almost see opponents rushing to the conflict in each of these earthly yet spiritual arenas. As in every athletic contest, there are heroes in each arena.

That is, in each generation particular heroes arise in football, soccer, baseball, tennis, or golf. They are often memorialized in some way so that succeeding young players may be encouraged to press on for victory and mastery.

Often, the abilities and methods of these heroes are carefully scrutinized. Their particular strokes or skills are dissected for the inspiration and utilization of succeeding players.

Biblically, there are three unique heroes whom God separates for a special place on His award stand. Their choice and naming by God twice in one passage in Ezekiel is most interesting. They are featured because of their righteousness and their ability to deliver themselves.

Actually, this section of Scripture in context concerns a coming judgment in which these men "...would deliver neither son nor daughter; they would deliver only themselves by their righteousness" (Ezekiel 14:20). God makes it clear in the passage that we should see and study their ways and their doings in reference to the ultimate conflict.

Giants of Conflict

And just who are these three giants of conflict, chosen heroes of God, that He would put in the arena against any foe, knowing their ability to overcome and persist in righteousness? The names Abraham, David, Samuel, or Samson might come to mind. But, no! God's heroic threesome includes *Noah, Daniel*, and *Job*, always in that order.

Are you surprised? It is especially amazing to find Daniel there, since he was basically a captive in Babylon and a contemporary of Ezekiel.

But, stop. When you look for a moment at their personal histories, the reasons for their selection become clear. *Noah* confronted a world system that was under the judgment of God, and he escaped. He endured by hearing and believing the Word of God against all the clamor and unbelief of the society of his day.

Daniel is particularly remembered for freedom from defilement and for his "excellent spirit," which persisted in obedience to God against all opposition, threat, and persecution.

Job, of course, survives as a vulnerable expose of Satan's accusation and of privilege in reference to the believer. His story provides an interesting backdrop for every believer's contest to fully enter into God's will and purpose over the enemy's subtle and sometimes extremely overt opposition.

Noah, Daniel, and Job — unique, irreplaceable, unrefutable champions against the world, the flesh, and the devil. Here, then, is a context for our study and an inspiration for our focus. How completely the Word of God prepares us!

Faith Challenges Continue

The writer of the book of Hebrews has especially captured the unique nature of conflict in the believer's struggle with spiritual faith and purpose. In his famous chapter on faith, he pictures each Bible character, known and unknown, as facing a specific challenge to belief and life-purpose.

Each was involved in choosing, going, standing, and confessing under intensely personal circumstances. Some had obvious and immediate visible confirmations of their faith in victory, while some obtained the fruit of victory in torture, persecution, and seeming defeat.

The writer reminds us, speaking both of great success and seeming failure:

And all these, having obtained a good testimony through faith, did not receive the promise,

God having provided something better for us, that they should not be made perfect apart from us.

Hebrews 11:39,40

The concept of these verses, as picked up in several translations, is that the heroes of the past had their names entered into the record book for their accomplishment, but the achievement recorded remains open, and the challenge continues down unto us!

Take courage! Not only is the conflict as real in your generation, but the potential for triumphant victory and overcoming reward also remains open. There are blank spaces in the biblical record of heroes of faith for your name!

Running With Endurance

The Hebrews writer continues:

Therefore we also, since we are surrounded by so great a cloud of witnesses, let us lay aside every weight and the sin which so easily ensnares us, and let us run with endurance the race that is set before us,

> looking unto Jesus, the author and finisher of our faith,
> who for the joy that was set before Him endured the cross,
> despising the shame, and has sat down at the right hand of
> the throne of God.
>
> **Hebrews 12:1,2**

Seldom is Scripture more vivid or applicable than in this chapter. Every believer has a personal contest, an *agona*, or an "agony" or "race."

A part of the contest involves the "chastening of the Lord" — a chastening which yields fruit to "those who have been trained by it." However, this chastening may also produce bitterness, profanity, or secularization in the spirit of those who respond negatively to it.

Our Source of Encouragement

There are many spectators in the stadium seats, their number so vast that they constitute that "great cloud of witnesses," which doubtless includes the previously mentioned heroes and heroines of faith.

But only Jesus is clearly seen by each contestant. His example, and the fact that He was the "first-goer" in every test of endurance, is an encouragement of incredible proportion to every other participant.

Like a modern Olympiad, the arenas or stadiums for the participants in these spiritual challenges will vary and change. Preliminary contests may be in one location; semifinals in another; and the final contests in a third.

For us, the struggle may sometimes be against the mindset of the world; at other times, we will face a battle in the flesh or spirit; or a conflict of direct involvement against our purpose by Satan. But every contest will have a discernible issue and specific stakes.

Believers must lay aside weights and the sin which so easily ensnares us. The author is reminding the Hebrew Christians and us that there are agonizing personal conflicts which form the only true path to spiritual reality and vital Christian experience.

Clearing the Track

These conflicts arise on two levels, the first of which is preparatory training before the actual contest, and secondly the conflict itself.

In the first level, we are striving against ourselves, putting away our own excess, as athletes rid themselves of superfluous flesh through severe training. And we must also clear the track of the sins which would trap and ensnare us, preventing a successful running of the race.

There are, therefore, issues of conflict and arenas in which we face them. But there also are heroes — spiritual victors and overcomers — to encourage us in our race.

"You are of God, little children," writes John, "and have overcome them, because He who is in you is greater than he who is in the world" (1 John 4:4).

CHAPTER 8

The World That's Too Much With Us

I was raised in a solid, evangelical atmosphere, but one which sometimes was stifling with legalism. All of this was done to keep the behavior of "the world" — a frightening specter of something "out there" which was dangerous and unknown — at bay.

What that world out there generated was known as "worldliness," which needed to be avoided like the plague or leprosy.

The Christian was, on this basis, often defined by extreme issues. Women fell particular target in almost every issue of style, clothing, and other feminine embellishments.

One person summed up this legalistic lifestyle by saying, "I don't eat, drink, smoke, or chew, or go with girls who do!" Quite an accomplishment, no doubt!

All this teaching made "the world" a mysterious, unknown place which got *more* alluring and attractive by the sermon. Curiosity seemed to be raised with every further slamming of some specific door which was identified with this realm.

I had never attended a movie until I was in junior high school, and my entire class attended "Quo Vadis." I couldn't sleep for nights, questioning even that decision.

In truth, I probably didn't miss much by not being in "the world," and I would probably have made sensible choices with such issues if temperance and not prohibition had been offered me.

The Enemy in Our Midst

But the most dangerous flaw of such teaching was that it left the true enemy often in our very homes and churches! "The world" is really never so cleverly enumerated and defined as we heard it.

What is this "world," the friendship of which is "enmity with God"? What system is this that is so anti-Christ that "Whoever therefore wants to be a friend of the world makes himself an enemy of God" (James 4:4)? Perhaps John gives us the best clue in First John 2:

> **Do not love the world or the things in the world. If anyone loves the world, the love of the Father is not in him.**
>
> **For all that is in the world — the lust of the flesh, the lust of the eyes, and the pride of life — is not of the Father but is of the world.**
>
> **And the world is passing away, and the lust of it; but he who does the will of God abides forever.**
>
> **1 John 2:15-17**

That might be simple, except the same, short letter states that:

- Jesus Christ is the propitiation "for the whole world" (1 John 2:2)
- Believers are to distribute "this world's goods" (1 John 3:17)
- "God has sent His only begotten Son into the world" (1 John 4:9)
- Believers are to be manifesting love and boldness like Christ "in this world" (1 John 4:17)

What Is "the World"?

Obviously, there are at least three clear and interchangeable biblical uses of the word "world." We must carefully understand each use from the context of the Scripture.

In the first place, "the world" may often mean "the physical and created universe."

Are believers to reject *that* world? Of course not, for it is a daily testimony to God's glory and handiwork, and we are to worship the Lord as Creator in proper stewardship of His workmanship. The physical world is, in fact, described as a *poiema* in Romans 1:19,20 — a poem, an artistic creation of God Himself!

Second, the Scriptures will often use "the world" to describe the world of mankind; the creation of God in humanity. Again we ask, "Should we avoid loving or being in contact with this world?"

Here the answer may appear more mixed. It is probably in this use that Jesus prayed, "I do not pray that you should take them out of the world, but that you should keep them from the evil one," and again, "as you sent Me into the world, I also have sent them into the world" (John 17:15,18)

This is the world which God "so loved that He gave His only begotten Son" (John 3:16) — the world for whose sins Christ became a propitiation.

It is an unfortunate truth, however, that most believers withdraw from the world of mankind, thinking that to be the demand of righteousness and obedience

Perhaps it is truer than we want to believe that evangelicals as a whole "love *souls* and hate *people.*" Individuals in the world seem to have no value apart from their "decisions" for God. And a weary and wary world often views the Christian as friendly only to the point of converting them, and thus pragmatic and insincere.

We must love the world of mankind in a sacrificial, redemptive manner, as did our Master, the Lord Jesus Christ.

What world, then, are we to hate, avoid, and have no friendship with? It is our third example: the system of thought and the aims, priorities, and slogans of that system which have reference only to this life.

This understanding falls generally but not entirely in the category of materialism. Ultimately, it involves the community and objects as well as principles of a system with allegiance and priorities related *only* to this world and this life. In contrast is the world to come and allegiance to Almighty God.

Materialism Slips Into the Church

The penetration of the materialistic system into our lives and thinking becomes obvious by the conversation and the maxims by which we live. Often this system is promoted even as a purpose or definition of the Christian life!

Several years ago, a chain letter was distributed among clergymen. It promised that if government bonds were sent to the top three names, and your name were added to the bottom of the list, you would eventually receive great wealth.

I knew many of these men. They were business-smart and intelligent. They knew that such a letter could not generate wealth, and that only the early participants would win, leaving others to lose their entire investment. Yet the plan became so extensive that denominational officials had to take action against their clergymen participating in the scheme!

"How can that be?" you ask incredulously. "Men committed to the Gospel involved in such obvious foolishness."

The answer is not so simple as it may appear. Do you remember when Ezra was leading a group back to Jerusalem to bring reform and restoration?

The Problem With Levites

After a three-day wait, a biblical time of full delay and testimony, they discovered that none of the sons of Levi were among them (Ezra 8:15). After all, Levites had no land inheritance. They probably fared better in captivity than in many periods of dependency upon the people of God!

Nehemiah later revealed, in fact, that the Levites' fears were well founded. In his day, the portions owed to them had not been paid by the people, and these ministers had to return to the fields to simply survive (Nehemiah 13:11,12)!

The lack of financial security in ministry seems to have a very long history. Haven't you heard these old maxims:

"No one will take care of you when you're old and gray."

"Every tub must sit on its own bottom."

"You need to get all you can, and can all you get."

"Another Gospel"

Acceptance of the slogans, fears, and priorities of the world is a very real issue in the church world. Various pyramid schemes of a "get-rich-quick" nature often turn to church groups and organizations for their greatest resource of potential customers. If you want to sell soap or government bonds, the church seems to provide a ready audience!

This is the world which is always at enmity with the cross and the true Gospel. It is, in fact, often taught as "another Gospel" with much of the enthusiasm and accompaniments of true religion. It is always focused on "the-here-and-now," as opposed to the "other" and "the ultimate."

It frequently mocks the "other worldliness" of biblical orientation. Life is defined in which we *possess*, and how we compare with others in the world is a seal of significance and importance. The heroes and heroines of the world system are possessors and users.

Following "The Royal Law"

James particularly counters this value system:

My brethren, do not hold the faith of our Lord Jesus Christ, the Lord of glory, with partiality.

For if there should come into your assembly a man with gold rings, in fine apparel, and there should also come in a poor man in filthy clothes,

and you pay attention to the one wearing the fine clothes and say to him, "You sit here in a good place," and say to the poor man, "Sit here at my footstool,"

have you not shown partiality among yourselves, and become judges with evil thoughts?

Listen, my beloved brethren: Has God not chosen the poor of this world to be rich in faith and heirs of the kingdom which He promised to those who love Him?

But you have dishonored the poor man. Do not the rich oppress you and drag you into the courts?

Do they not blaspheme that noble name by which you are called?

If you really fulfill the royal law according to the Scripture, "You shall love your neighbor as yourself," you do well;

but if you show partiality, you commit sin, and are convicted by the law as transgressors.

James 2:1-9

The world system directly opposes the Word and the will of the Father. When we fix our attention and affection on worldly objects — on what the world can give or furnish us — we soon become possessed by the spirit which lives only for this moment.

The Way of Escape

We can only escape this influence through the Word of God. As Peter wrote:

as His divine power has given to us all things that pertain to life and godliness, through the knowledge of Him who called us by glory and virtue,

by which have been given to us exceedingly great and precious promises, that through these you may be partakers of the divine nature, having escaped the corruption that is in the world through lust.

2 Peter 1:3,4

You can readily see in this and many other Scriptures that the battleground between the world vs. the Word and the will of Father God is the mind of man. That's where the struggle with slogans, affection, and priorities is really waged!

Peter had earlier urged his readers to "gird up," or "brace up" their *minds* by putting attention on "...the grace that is to be brought to you at the revelation of Jesus Christ" (1 Peter 1:13).

Having the Mind of Christ

As believers, we are to possess the mind, or mental attitude and disposition, which was in Jesus Christ (Philippians 2:5). This was a spirit of releasing position and influence in order, as a servant, to fulfill the will of the Father in humility and obedience.

This spirit of Christ is one of self-forgetfulness and denial which sees the Redemption in a cross, and is willing to be emptied and even to accept the death of reputation for higher and more eternal purposes.

Again, *the prevailing attitude of the world system is possessing, controlling, and accumulating. It is never the mind of Christ.*

We must make a choice between the two, because *we become what we dwell on mentally.* The relation to what we think and what we become is taught in many places in Scripture. See Proverbs 12:7, Mark 7:18-23, Second Corinthians 10:5, and so forth.

Satan's View of Mankind

It would be an interesting study to spend time with Jesus' so-called wilderness temptation. Remember, this trial took place *after* His great water baptism with the resulting public affirmation from the Father.

Satan's appeal is always to man's appetite. He places man only upon a material basis. Accordingly, in Satan's view, man's lust and highest ambition would always be to satisfy the natural, material appetite, not the spiritual.

"Worship," Satan seems to say, "is possible from man only selfishly, with a desire to possess, leaving no place for service."

I wonder if Jesus' entire wilderness temptation experience was not designed by Satan to prove beyond question that humanity was completely unworthy of Redemption.

Jesus' answers were not only a victory in His own humanity over temptation; they were an eloquent statement of faith in man. Mankind *is* capable of intelligent consideration of the ways of God. Man doesn't trust God only instinctively, worshipping to gain possessions.

By the exercise of his faith, intelligence, and willpower, man can be surrounded by the material, and can even be capable of seeking or using material things without allowing them to hinder his spiritual interests.

How Satan Tempted Jesus

All of us can identify immediately with the three levels of attack Satan used against Jesus. He first attacked the will of God for Christ, and then attempted to misuse the Word of God and misdirect worship.

In this instance, physical hunger was an element in the economy of the Father's process. Jesus was hungry because He was doing God's will. Because Jesus' hunger was natural, Satan suggested a natural route to satisfaction.

"Use your sonship," Satan seemed to be saying — revealing his attitude that the privilege of sonship is selfish gratification. The will of God is thus made to appear unreasonable!

Jesus' answer was from Deuteronomy 8:3, which reads:

So He humbled you, allowed you to hunger, and fed you with manna...that He might make you know that man shall not live by bread alone; but man lives by every word that proceeds from the mouth of the Lord.

Do you understand this argument? For Christ to have made bread of the stones would have violated the will of

God. But by waiting on the Father, He knew the bread would ultimately be given. No wonder Jesus later says to the disciples, "I have food to eat of which you do not know...My food is to do the will of Him who sent me, and to finish His work" (John 4:32,34).

The world system — the material — not only concerns the will of the Father, but the issues of the Word of God and worship, as we see in the continuation of Jesus' wilderness trial.

The system of prevailing emphasis on comfort and material success often resorts to misapplied Scripture and self-directed worship to emphasize its prevailing attitudes and goals. Like Jesus, we must also see the battle nature of this conflict.

To worship God in sincerity is to accept God's will for service and His judgment of ultimate and eternal values.

CHAPTER 9

Learning From Noah

Bill Cosby, the American humorist, has a wonderful skit concerning a conversation between God and Noah. In it, Noah is constantly stopping God with questions, because he doesn't understand the language God is using.

"What's a *flood?* How does it *rain?* Whoever saw an *ark?*" and so forth. Perhaps the skit is more real than comedy.

Noah had to trust the word he received from God. He had absolutely no way to confirm its reality in his material experience, because it had never yet rained upon the earth!

Haven't you wondered about heaven and hell? Jesus Christ was constantly teaching that everyone will live forever in one or another state. But one can neither prove nor disprove heaven or hell by logical, pragmatic means, any more than a babe in the womb can explain the outside world.

Faith is not sight. In fact, it is often carried out in stubborn confrontation with the "real" and the material. Biblical hope is waiting with courage and perseverance for what we do *not* see.

Faith is the true ground support of things hoped for. Anyone who has established a true, genuine, personal relationship with God comes to know, at least in moments, by flashes, a quality of experience which does not fit into the material world's boundaries of time and space.

There is a bottom-line logic for believers, according to the writer of Hebrews. Believers understand that seen and material things exist out of the invisible through the Word of God.

The atomic and nuclear revolutions may have proved the point, but the real conclusion is still in the spiritual. God's Word — what He says about reality, priority, and purpose — is the everlasting. The rest is as transitory as summer flowers.

Real "Worldliness"

Real "worldliness" is a so-called "realistic" attitude toward security and existence; in other words, toward the *now,* which keeps a person from complete and total trust in God.

Man believes in the continuation of all things "as they were from the beginning." We like to believe it's a stable universe!

In Noah's day, as in our own, life seems totally consumed with the affairs of this life. Jesus made this attitude and its resulting dulling of spiritual insight and perception a comparison between Noah's day, His own and, ours (Matthew 24:37-39 and Luke 17:26,27).

Everything that surrounds the believer seems to call for his emphasis on the issues of the material. Indeed, it always is as it was in the days of Noah!

As we have seen, the battle between this world system and the Word and the will of God comes in through our mind. As in the famous Greek diatribes, the opponent tries to "rub through" the argument of the other and replace his argument or reasoning with his own. That is doubtless the context of Paul's famous statement in Second Corinthians 10:4,5:

> **For the weapons of our warfare are not carnal but mighty in God for pulling down strongholds,**
>
> **casting down arguments and every high thing that exalts itself against the knowledge of God, bringing every thought into captivity to the obedience of Christ.**

Under Strategic Attack

The true knowledge of God, involving an inevitable value system differing from the world's, will always be under strategic attack from the enemy.

The world will attempt to create by fantasy supposed needs and hungers which will compromise and ultimately control and cripple the believer.

No wonder God hates that world system of thought! It is in every way at *enmity* to the purposes of God. A victory over the world must include, as well as discipline and self-control, the element of divine transformation.

I love the J. B. Phillips translation of Romans 12:1,2:

With eyes wide open to the mercies of God, I beg you, my brothers, as an act of intelligent worship, to give him your bodies, as a living sacrifice, consecrated to him and acceptable by him.

***Don't let the world around you squeeze you into its own mold,* but let God remold your minds from within, so that you may prove in practice that the plan of God for you is good, meets all his demands and moves toward the goal of true maturity.**

The Scriptural explanations of Noah's victory over the world are fantastic. The ark he built escaped the judgment from the world system. The writer to the Hebrews says:

By faith Noah, being divinely warned of things not yet seen, moved with godly fear, prepared an ark for the saving of his household, by which he condemned the world and became heir of the righteousness which is according to faith.

Hebrews 11:7

It is not wrong to say that "fear" here means actually "to grasp or take hold of something circumspectly," and "warning" is as well translated "divine instruction."

Noah grasped the true reality, the spiritual dimension, of his age. The very fact that he did, proves that this ability *is* possible to man. Thus, it stands as a witness or judgment on the rest of the world. *The same ark and Gospel which saves also condemns!*

The Genesis account simply records that Noah has "found grace in the eyes of the Lord," but that choice was *not*

accidental. God later explains, "I have seen that you are right-
eous before Me in this generation" (Genesis 6:8; 7:1).

A Believer's Intolerance

A part of the believer's wrestling with the world system
revolves around a seeming intolerance or "one-way-ness" of
true faith and the Gospel itself.

The world always argues for acceptance. Everything is
beautiful in its own way, the world says. Everyone has a right
to be or do as he chooses. Even faith is to be according to the
dictates of each person's conscience, the world argues.

How difficult is the divine revelation of Scripture! It
states that there is *a way* revealed by God and there is *no other
way*.

Noah learned from God and God alone the origin,
character, and destiny of the earth and man. He believed
God's system of knowledge, and he was not influenced by
frail human theories. Noah accepted what God said the
world was like, and he believed what God said would ultimately happen.

In reality, the only eternal knowledge is the Bible, the
revealed Word of God. The believer learns at Calvary about
the world, man's sin, and God's Son.

*I must come to know in reality what kind of God came into
our world and what kind of a world God came into.* If I lose the
battle of the Word in my mind, the inevitable surrender to the
philosophy of the world will be obvious and inevitable.

Our "Escape Craft"

Grace and fear are the symbols of the believer's shield of
faith. Noah's ark is constructed of the same spiritual elements
that our current "escape craft" needs in order to "escape the
corruption that is in the world" (2 Peter 1:4).

God's Word is the sword of the Spirit and our mightiest
bulwark and defense against evil. Like any sailor or pilot, we

must take care concerning this craft — God's Word — which will provide our escape from destruction.

The greatest weapon in the hand of Satan is the Word of God wrested *out of context* and *handled deceitfully* (2 Corinthians 4:1-4). Jesus in His wilderness temptation shows us the most beautiful respect for the proper interpretation and application of holy Scriptures.

Jesus also gave great importance to a person's thought life. He rebuked the fear of the disciples when the Pharisees and scribes judged them for eating with unwashed hands.

"Oh, are you as dull as they are?" he said. "Can't you see that anything that goes into a man from outside cannot make him 'common' or unclean? You see, it doesn't go into his heart, but into his stomach, and passes out of the body altogether, so that all food is clean enough. "But," he went on, "whatever comes out of a man, that is what makes a man 'common' or unclean. *For it is from inside, from men's hearts and minds, that evil thoughts arise* — lust, theft, murder, adultery, greed, wickedness, deceit, sensuality, envy, slander, arrogance and folly! All these evil things come from inside a man and make him unclean!

Mark 7:18-23 J. B. Phillips (italics added)

Basic Building Blocks

The mind is the trigger of man's rational personality, and each thought is a basic building block of every ultimate decision, experience, or fantasy.

As we saw in Second Corinthians 10:4,5, the world system attempts to constantly replace God's true and ultimate knowledge with "imposing defense" and material substitutes.

We must fight to control our thinking, capturing every thought and forcing our whole mind to acknowledge the authority of Jesus Christ.

The name "disciple" means "a disciplined learner." Escaping the thought-control of a world system is no small struggle! It's a real battleground and a major arena in the Christian life.

The Elders Rested

According to Hebrews 11, the faith of the elders rested on their confidence in the spoken word of God. After all, they reasoned, *everything material came into being from the invisible, through just such a word of God* (Hebrews 11:3):

By faith we understand that the worlds were framed by the word of God, so that the things which are seen were not made of things which are visible.

Therefore, when God said, "Leave your country, conceive seed, offer your son, refuse Pharaoh's court, forsake Egypt, and so forth" they obeyed, believing the greater power and reward to be in God's word, not in material circumstances.

We know from the record that these were not perfect people or superstars. They schemed in tight places. They often went the wrong way. Sometimes they acted on bad advice. They knew experiences of intense fear and anxiety. But, like Noah, those in the Hall of Faith persisted ultimately *in obedience to the word of God despite society's opposition.*

Noah's conflict lasted at least 110 years! He is God's hero concerning this material, worldly system, because he is the ultimate example of believing both in his ability to hear God's voice *and* in God's ultimate truthfulness.

CHAPTER 10

The Flesh: A Good Way To Spell SELF Backwards

Charles Schulz, the creator of the world-famous "Peanuts" comic strip, often uses his humor to expose deep personal meanings within life.

One of my favorite strips shows poor Charlie Brown coming home from a ball game, terribly disillusioned.

"One hundred and forty to nothing!" he is heard to exclaim. "I just don't understand it. We were so sincere!"

How often that simple statement expresses the believer's dilemma. "We have met the enemy," one general reported to his superiors, "and it is us!"

I cannot be overly objective about my problems, since I am inextricably involved in them myself. Barbra Streisand, the American songstress, sang a haunting song on an early album:

Where am I going? Why should I care?

No matter where I run, I meet myself there.

Looking inside me, what do I see?

Anger and hope and doubt.

What am I all about, and where am I going?

I am a mixture — a little bit of heaven and a whole lot of earth — in love with God and pursuing holiness, but very alive in a body which is not yet redeemed.

Flesh vs. Spirit

Biblically, the dichotomy which we experience is called "the flesh vs. the spirit." And as the Apostle Paul writes:

For the flesh lusts against the Spirit, and the Spirit against the flesh; and these are contrary to one another, so that you do not do the things that you wish.

Galatians 5:17

Again, within the arena of the flesh, we need some definition of terms. "Flesh" can mean the animal creation, meat, non-bone structure of man, body as distinguished from spirit, human nature, natural or physical origin, or man's sensuous nature with cravings which excite to sin.

We could spend a chapter on Scripture references alone! But for our present purposes, let us see the flesh as the human or earthly nature of man apart from divine influence. It is prone to sin and includes the weaker, lowly, and more sensuous nature of man, often tending to ungodliness and generally opposed to God.

The Stadium of Our Conflict

It is, however, a part of us, an arena of our discipleship, a stadium of our conflict. There is one sense in which the flesh is without, or external to, one's life, but an even greater sense in which it is within.

Like a radio or television set, the *receiver* is in our home, but the *programming* is most often controlled by outside agents! Our choice is therefore dependent on the will to turn it off, or change the channel! That is uppermost in the issue of flesh. *The flesh cannot always be seen as sinful; often it simply is passing, corruptible, non-eternal.*

For he who sows to his flesh will of the flesh reap corruption [decaying matter], but he who sows to the Spirit will of the Spirit reap everlasting life.

Galatians 6:8

The context of this passage shows the issue to be the choice of words and time investment, with eternal reward in mind.

CHAPTER 11

Daniel 10: Lions' Zip

Recently we have heard a great deal about hostages. Generally these are people held in bondage by groups trying to get their causes acknowledged by governments.

Many hostages are treated cruelly, and some are even killed. Their plight is even more difficult because they ultimately have nothing to do with the reasons for their imprisonment.

Daniel was actually such a hostage. He was taken prisoner along with a few other young princes in the first warning wave of captivity that came to his nation, Judah.

Although the instrument of this event was the great power of Babylon, under its phenomenal leader Nebuchadnezzar, the actual power behind Judah's captivity was God Himself!

The Jews had rejected the warnings of the Lord. Among their sins of idolatry and forsaking God's law, they had failed for 490 years to keep the Sabbath of the land!

Daniel: A Time Clock for Judgment

Through the prophet Jeremiah, therefore, God spoke to Judah of a coming seventy-year captivity. Daniel's bondage was actually the beginning of this fulfillment of prophecy. His life is like a time clock for the judgment. It is his prayers and intercession which herald the end of the dealings of God in the so-called Babylonian captivity.

In the first year of Darius...I, Daniel, understood by the books the number of the years specified by the word of the

Lord, given through Jeremiah the prophet, that He would accomplish seventy years in the desolations of Jerusalem.

Then I set my face toward the Lord God to make request by prayer and supplications, with fasting, sackcloth, and ashes.

Daniel 9:1-3

Daniel's Spiritual Integrity

Thus, Daniel is an ultimate example of one who wins a victory over the flesh. Wrenched away from his family, home and nation, he wages a continuing and successful battle to continue in his spiritual integrity.

Every Sunday School child knows how Daniel refused to defile himself and how, later in life, he refused to bow to compromise in his worship of Almighty God. For this, he was thrown into the lions' den! Many know further that Daniel was a prophet (Matthew 24:15), and that he had great insight into God's purposes.

The truth is that Daniel ultimately served four important world rulers as their most trusted adviser, yet he never compromised his ultimate commitment to the lordship of Jehovah in his life.

The Flesh: A Warring King

The flesh, as we have seen, is like a warring king and kingdom which wage constant war for control of the believer's strength and destiny. How can we be victorious when the struggle is often so intense? (See James 4:1-4.)

The writer to the Hebrews describes the Christian experience as a race, or "agony," which demands discipline and endurance (Hebrews 12:1-4).

The first two components in this discipline are: (1) to lay aside superfluous weight, trimming our life into proper strength, and (2) to deal with the besetting sin which lies constantly around our feet, waiting to ensnare us and trip us up.

We are to continually look to Jesus:

> **For consider Him who endured such hostility from sin-
> ners against Himself, lest you become weary and discour-
> aged in your souls.**
>
> **You have not yet resisted to bloodshed, striving against
> sin.**
>
> **Hebrews 12:3,4**

The words "resisted" and "striving" are extremely
strong words in the original language.

Clearly, the two targets of the flesh against the believer
are in the arena of the physical body and the human spirit.
Daniel, whose name meant "God is my Judge," was immediately attacked in both of these areas, as every believer will be.

In the first test, Daniel purposed in his heart that he
would not defile himself (Daniel 1:8). In the second test, it
could be said of him after many hostile attacks, "...Daniel
distinguished himself...because an excellent spirit was in
him..." (Daniel 6:3).

It is apparent from Daniel's life why the Holy Spirit
would see him as an ultimate champion of righteousness
(Ezekiel 14:14).

Principles of Standing and Overcoming

There are, I believe, specific teachings of standing and
overcoming against the flesh that can be discerned from the
life and experience of Daniel. Let us examine these seven
principles in the following pages.

Principle One

*Daniel submitted to the timing and historical placement of his
life without bitterness.*

People are often heard to say, "I didn't ask to be born!"
or "I had nothing to do with this — that's just the way it is."

Others often express the wish to have lived in another
age, and will even refer to themselves as being "ahead of their
time." There is no question that each generation faces unique

tests and unrepeatable circumstances. The world at every specific age will present unique challenges to the believer.

Think of the Christians who lived during the years of Roman persecution, those who lived in Nazi Germany, or those who lived under Communist regimes.

But in the New Testament, the Greek word generally translated "persecution" is *thlipsis*, which is better understood as "pressure." We all understand that!

The flesh may or may not bring us to the point of physical torture or martyrdom, but it *always* presses in upon us with incredible pressure!

If anyone ever could have bemoaned his circumstances in life, it would have been Daniel. Taken as a token captive, he had to serve in a foreign land, while the rest of his people went on with their normal lives back in Judah during the next twenty years.

Daniel was, in fact, a hostage of the Babylonian government and king. Although he lived the remainder of his life without seeing his homeland again, Daniel served God faithfully and without compromise, winning the respect and admiration of four separate monarchs. He not only lived through their four regimes; he survived the downfall of two of these kingdoms.

No wonder the Holy Spirit ends the book of Daniel with this promise:

But you, go your way till the end; for you shall rest, and will arise to your inheritance at the end of the days.

Daniel 12:13

So each of us has been born into different circumstances, and each of us has widely differing abilities and physical or mental limitations. We live in a specific generation or era, and we must work out the lordship of Jesus Christ in our own unique cultural setting.

Accepting our plight and finding every opportunity within it to work for the furtherance of the Gospel frees us from the bitterness and negativity which plays into the hand of the flesh. Oh, to be able to say, with the Apostle Paul:

...the things which happened to me have actually turned out for the furtherance of the gospel.

Philippians 1:12

Principal Two

Daniel possessed a correct sense of self-image, and he considered all his life and circumstance a gift from God.

There is no doubt that Daniel started life with some real advantages. The Chaldeans used a checklist from Nebuchadnezzar when they chose Daniel and the other hostages.

The hostages they selected were either kings' descendants or young nobles with these qualifications:

young men in whom there was no blemish, but good-looking, gifted in all wisdom, possessing knowledge and quick to understand....

Daniel 1:4

Perhaps you, like me, sometimes look in the mirror and wonder if God made a mistake! However, in a sense, Daniel's unique qualifications were his passport into bondage.

Once in Babylon, the young Israeli captives faced their first serious challenge. Their captors, although friendly and generous, immediately attempted to change their names: Daniel to Belteshazzar, Hananiah to Shadrach, Mishael to Meshach, and Azariah to Abed-Nego.

"Simple," you say. "The Babylonians probably found the Hebrew names hard to pronounce, so they gave them names in their own language."

Perhaps. That certainly was not an unusual practice among immigrants. But at least note what the changes entailed: Each of the Hebrew lads had a specific Hebrew name which praised an aspect of Jehovah and His goodness. Their newly assigned names all were an expression of the worship of a heathen god or goddess of Babylon!

An early task of the flesh in its warfare against us is to compromise the true nature of God within us. It is God who has made us to differ, and it is He who has given each of us a unique talent or gift in our life. Even our physical and mental differences are a gift from God and must be understood as such (1 Corinthians 4:7).

One of the earliest attacks upon us, therefore, will be to "rub away" the true knowledge of God within us concerning our life and purpose. Our enemy will attempt to substitute another concept concerning our self, our life, or our purpose, and this concept will be foreign to Jehovah.

We have already briefly studied Second Corinthians 10:3-5 in this regard. I simply remind you, at this point, of the manner in which the Greek word *diatribe* allowed one speaker to totally eliminate the reasoning or argument of the other, and to substitute his own.

Strangely, in the story of Daniel, his three companions appear to have accepted their new names, but Daniel persisted in claiming the identity of his spiritual heritage. Perhaps it's simply coincidence or editorial privilege, but I am inclined to believe that Daniel resisted this effort to compromise or confuse his identity.

I can almost hear Daniel say, "I may be a captive in a strange land, and I will learn to serve and benefit my circumstance — but I will never forget or compromise who I am by the work of Jehovah. As God is my judge, Daniel is who I will be until I die."

Principle Three

Daniel made specific decisions concerning obedience and spiritual conscience which enabled the release of God's enlightenment and revelation through him.

The flesh literally surrounds us, and its impact is to ultimately close us off from perceiving spiritual reality.

John wrote, "Look to yourselves, that we do not lose those things we worked for, but that we may receive a full reward" (Second John 8).

The flesh exalts in the physical and the material. It only acknowledges that which is visible; it is blind to invisible reality. That's why faith, as described in Hebrews 11:1-4, is not faith in the *unknown* — far from it! God's wonderful truths *can* be known. The faith found in Hebrews 11 is faith in the *unseen!*

A specific lesson in the battle against the flesh is that there will always be some specific decision on our part which enables spiritual light to penetrate and spiritual revelation to begin.

"But Daniel purposed in his heart that he would not defile himself with the portion of the king's delicacies...." This is certainly not a statement for some sort of diet restriction to be impressed on those who would be spiritual.

Daniel knew the issues were being drawn: The Babylonians wanted to change his name and further compromise him into the ease and attraction of their lifestyle. It was time to take a stand.

These people needed to know the strength of his purpose and his faith. Daniel was not normally recalcitrant: The fact that he eventually served four separate kings proves that. But now he knew the time had come to make a decision that would decide his destiny.

The Psalmist wrote, "The secret of the Lord is with them that fear Him," and Daniel's choice was to exhibit the fear of the Lord over the control of the flesh through the Babylonians.

No one can decree the specific areas of choice and decision for each believer. To try to dictate them would produce bondage and legalism. But every believer must make early, decisive choices to stand *against* the flesh and to give spiritual reality first place in his life.

Perhaps Daniel's experience under King Josiah in Judah had finalized his commitment to absolute choice against the flesh. Probably no king since David showed greater affection for God or offered more promise of spiritual renewal in the state of Judah. Yet, Josiah was lifted up to do a presumptuous and foolish thing without God's direction. This resulted in his tragic death (2 Chronicles 34-35).

Daniel's almost rigid stand over a specific issue in the flesh — his specific obedience — began a pattern of release of God's enlightenment in his life. Perhaps God is waiting for a specific decision on *your* part to bring about such a release and victory for you!

Principle Four

Daniel was committed to the biblical principle of trinity fellowship (koinonia).

Even a casual reader of Scripture notes a simple, unique pattern of victory. God the Father has planned that one of the most effective experiences the believer has is to live out transparent and intimate fellowship with a few significant others.

Daniel is constantly associated with Azariah, Mishael, and Hananiah. Jesus Christ Himself was most intimate with Peter, James, and John in His more difficult or rewarding moments. In fact, when Jesus prayed at the end of His life that the believers might be one, it was a oneness personified in a particular example:

> **that they all may be one, as You, Father, are in Me, and I in You; that they also may be one in Us, that the world may believe that You sent Me.**

> **John 17:21**

There are so many biblical examples or specific statements concerning this principle. None is more thorough than Ecclesiastes 4:9-12, where the wisdom is shared for us:

> **Two are better than one, because they have a good reward for their labor.**

> **For if they fall, one will lift up his companion. But woe to him who is alone when he falls, for he has no one to help him up.**

> **Again, if two lie down together, they will keep warm; but how can one be warm alone?**

> **Though one may be overpowered by the other, two can withstand him. And a threefold cord is not quickly broken.**

Throughout the Gospel accounts, Jesus always sent forth the disciples in teams, generally by two's; and the subsequent New Testament Church always responded in the same way to such calls of ministry.

Specifically, because such fellowship echoes the "Trinity relationship," there are great promises of multiplied blessing inherent in it.

For example, Deuteronomy 32:30 repeats negatively a promise given to Israel in Leviticus 26:8, a promise that by working in close, intimate brotherhood and fellowship, they would multiply their effectiveness: "How can one chase a thousand, and two put ten thousand to flight..." (Deuteronomy 32:30).

The experience of Jonathan and his armorbearers, among others, illustrates the truth of that fact. There will be ten times the effectiveness when we walk openly, transparently, with brothers and sisters.

Obviously, a study of this principle is a subject for a book itself. Every spiritual renewal in history has had this principle at its core. This includes the circle of twelve in the Wesleyan renewal, and the cottage prayer meetings in the 20th century.

Major ministries working with alcoholics and other addicted persons have found the only solution is in the forming of team relationships — each helping the other against the common enemy.

When Nebuchadnezzar threatened the wise men of the land with imminent death because they could not tell him both his dream *and* its interpretation, the Bible says:

> **Then Daniel went to his house, and made the decision known to Hananiah, Mishael, and Azariah, his companions,**
>
> **that they might seek mercies from the God of heaven concerning this secret....**
>
> **Daniel 2:17,18**

The word "companions" used in this passage is from a Hebrew word "to join or to compact." They weren't just roommates! There was a bonding of their lives and spirits which enabled them to be victorious over the surroundings of their captivity.

Is there such a "compact" in your life? If you were to fall, would anyone know where to look for you? The battle against the flesh is real and daily. One of God's most effective tools and graces for your life is this understanding.

Why not find someone and begin such a contract of fellowship immediately. I'm sure you'll begin to see the victories which Daniel did.

Principle Five

Daniel both understood and operated within his specific gift ministry.

Our Lord Jesus Christ specifically referred to Daniel as "the prophet" (Matthew 24:15; Mark 13:14). Although many modern perspectives of Daniel differ from that, I prefer to hold to that understanding.

The Bible record clearly shows Daniel operating within gifts of wisdom, interpretation and, ultimately, revelation and prophecy. In a unique psalm to God, Daniel declares:

Blessed be the name of God forever and ever, for wisdom and might are His.

And He changes the times and the seasons; He removes kings and raises up kings; He gives wisdom to the wise and knowledge to those who have understanding.

He reveals deep and secret things; He knows what is in the darkness, and light dwells with Him.

Daniel 2:20-22

Daniel closes his praise-note by saying:

I thank You and praise You, O God of my fathers; You have given me wisdom and might....

Daniel 2:23

Daniel used his gift to serve King Nebuchadnezzar as ruler over the whole province of Babylon and chief administrator over the wise men of Babylon. He later was third ruler in the kingdom under Belshazzar, and "prospered in the reign of Darius and in the reign of Cyrus the Persian" (Daniel 6:28).

Perhaps the most difficult thing we have to do in life is to discover our gifting spiritually and operate within that calling. Our society often holds us up to so many diverse expectations that we are debilitated.

I cannot do or be everything, but I *am* something. *Discovering God's gifting in my life and operating within its realm is a great safeguard against the flesh.*

There is such a variety of gifts and ministries: teaching, exhorting, giving, leading, showing mercy, hospitality, as well as the big five named in Ephesians 4:11! (See Ephesians 4, Romans 12, First Corinthians 12.)

When we know our gifting, we are to "wait on it," developing it by discipline, study, and prayer. Daniel waited on his gifting by carefully studying the prophets; particularly Jeremiah. (See Jeremiah 25:8-14 and 26:1-10 and compare with Daniel 9:2,3.)

It is generally believed that Daniel's last major activity was to negotiate with Cyrus the decrees of liberation for the Jews. Doubtless, he effectively brought to Cyrus' attention what God had forsworn concerning him nearly two centuries before! (See Isaiah 44:28-46.)

What a blessing to spend a life divinely focused in purpose and destiny.

Principle Six

Daniel both accepted and committed himself to a biblical and prophetic perspective of history.

The work and activity of the flesh always operates within the arena of the material. As the human, earthly nature of men, it finds attraction and reality in that which is seen, felt, and known through the physical.

We have already studied the believer's battle between the material, world-age concept of truth and reality vs. spiritually discerned realities.

According to Hebrews 11:3:

By faith we understand that the worlds were framed by the word [*rhema*, not *logos*] of God, so that the things which are seen were not made of things which are visible.

The flesh counts that as nonsense. In truth, every hero of faith had to operate within this realm, so that what God told him to do was *more real* and ultimate than the great material powers and events which surrounded him.

Daniel was constantly surrounded by the material grandeur of two of the greatest ancient kingdoms of all time — the Babylonian and the Medo-Persian empires. He must have enjoyed their blessings as a highly placed and rewarded civil servant, yet he never saw those material kingdoms as ultimate power. A simple reading of Daniel 2, Daniel 6, and Daniel 9 will demonstrate this fact.

Certainly no physical reality could be more pressuring or ultimate than a den of hungry lions! Yet Daniel perceived and committed himself to a concept of truth and reality seen in God and through His Word.

Because of that, Daniel could clearly see the continuing failure of man's subsequent governments, and predict the coming Messiah and His ultimate victory and kingdom.

The flesh is always weakened when we stand on the truth that "...the things which are seen are temporary, but the things which are not seen are eternal" (2 Corinthians 4:18).

Principle Seven

Daniel both understood and committed himself to intercession as God's appointed method of accomplishing His purpose in the world.

Dropping the last letter of the word "flesh" and spelling it backwards gives us "self." Flesh is the emphasis on human, physical, and non-spiritual matters of man. It is man's sensuous nature, without any suggestion necessarily of depravity or sexual desire.

Flesh operates within that which can be tasted, felt, touched, seen, or heard. The spirit of man, however, is equipped to perceive God and the realities of the unseen world.

The equipment of manipulation in the flesh are tools of force, appeal, and temptation. How much different are the weapons of spiritual warfare. They are "not carnal but mighty in God for pulling down strongholds" (2 Corinthians 10:4)

Prayer and intercession are God's chosen tracks upon which His fulfillment runs. Daniel thoroughly understood that.

It was not enough that Daniel saw in the prophecy the projected end of the captivity. He did not sit back, fold his arms, and say, "Well, I wonder how God will accomplish this?"

Scripture records, instead:

Then I set my face toward the Lord God to make request by prayer and supplications, with fasting, sackcloth, and ashes.

Daniel 9:3

A thorough reading of Daniel 9 will show you both the intensity and the method of Daniel's intercession.

The principles of intercession are another study. There are books in the recommended reading list at the end of this book to help you. Basically, intercession is to pray what is on the heart and mind of God, rather than our own "shopping list."

This enables us to participate in God's purpose and will for our lives, our families, our nation, and our world. Through intercession, we do heavenly warfare and release revelation! (See Daniel 9:20 through chapter 12.)

Above all, for our present purpose, the practice of intercession keeps our focus on the *real* world of the unseen and the spiritual, and thus frustrates and eliminates the tyranny of the flesh.

The Arena of Our Problems Made by Satan

Iremember once writing out some teaching transparencies to use with an overhead projector. My time was very limited, and I was writing quickly, using special pens to mark these celluloid sheets.

There wasn't time to check my spelling carefully, and that was a mistake! Imagine the amusement of the audience when one of the transparencies was flashed up on the huge screen, and I had spelled "Satan" with an "i," making it "Satin"! There may be only one letter difference in spelling, but it's a world of difference in truth! Satan is no soft, silky, attractive vision.

The truth is, many believers have a mythological view of the devil. They imagine him in horns and a tail, carrying a pitchfork when, in reality, he is a cunning, powerful, and dangerous adversary.

Satan knows our weaknesses and flaws, and he knows how to use them to his advantage to bring the work of God through the believer to a halt.

Satan's Limitations

The Bible clearly teaches that Satan is a limited created being who is in no way equal to God. He is not omnipotent, which means he does not have all power; he is not omniscient, he does not know everything; and he is not omnipresent, he cannot be everywhere at the same time.

He is, however, in charge of a world system of principalities and powers, including even rulers of this present age and its darkness, and spiritual hosts of wickedness in the heavenlies (Ephesians 6:12). No small armada, that!

Christians often blame Satan for things they are responsible for themselves. The Scriptures teach, "Each one is tempted, when he is drawn away by his own desires and enticed" (James 1:14). There is no doubt, however, that the darkness of this age contributes *to* one's temptation.

What Satan Can't Do

But *Satan cannot cause you to backslide,* and he cannot send anyone to hell, since he himself is a candidate, not a ruler, in that place. He cannot change God's mind about you (Zechariah 3:2). He cannot tempt you above what you are able to bear, send you to hell, or cause God to give up on you (Philippians 1:6).

There is no way Satan can forcibly stop you individually or the Church collectively from the outside. He has been immobilized by the victory of the Lord Jesus Christ, who, "Having disarmed principalities and powers, He made a public spectacle of them, triumphing over them in it" (Colossians 2:15).

Therefore, *the only weapons Satan has to use against us are the ones we ourselves give him!*

And Satan cannot touch you without the express permission of God. Job stands in the Bible as an ultimate example of Satan's attempt to discredit and defeat a believer.

We see in that most ancient of all stories the strange authority and permissions of the enemy, yet, above all, his strict limits of operation and the ultimate redeeming purpose of God in even allowing his attack against the believer.

Satan in the Arena

We have earlier examined Satan as a direct source of the Christian's problems. In this chapter we see Satan as one of the big three biblical arenas in which the believer meets his problems: (1) the world, (2) the flesh, and (3) the devil.

Whereas in the earlier chapter we saw the enemy as an opponent, we see in this brief study that he designs an entire "stadium" around his strategies to keep the believer from his effectiveness.

In her excellent devotional commentary on the book of Ephesians, Ruth Paxson says, "In light of Ephesians Satan will attempt three things: to despoil the Christian of his wealth; to decoy the Christian from his walk; and to disable the Christian from his warfare."

What Satan Can Do

We have seen what Satan *can't* do, but we must also acknowledge the arenas in which he *can* work. The New Testament teaches that Satan can:

1. Weaken our resistance through the flesh (1 Peter 2:11; James 4:1)
2. Ruin our defenses through entanglements (2 Timothy 2:4)
3. Eliminate our effectiveness through softness and compromise (2 Timothy 2:3)
4. Use his arsenal to accuse the believer and bring him into condemnation

The last of these four is doubtless Satan's most successful tool!

Lessons From Job

The experience of Job shows us how cleverly the enemy attacks the motive of the believer. Satan taunts God:

Does Job fear God for nothing?

Have You not made a hedge around him, around his household, and around all that he has on every side? You have blessed the work of his hands, and his possessions have increased in the land.

But now, stretch out Your hand and touch all that he has, and he will surely curse You to Your face!

Job 1:9-11

This is identical to the approach Satan shows Jesus in the wilderness temptation: Man only serves God instinctively to receive material blessings and provisions; he is incapable of serving God with will and purpose, seeking only to glorify the Lord.

The story of Job is not an easy one, and an interpreter must teach carefully from its total context. Although Job was "blameless and upright, and one who feared God and shunned evil..." (Job 1:1), he had a lot to learn.

What Job Learned

His repentance and restoration, recorded in Job 42, show an amazing amount of learning through the process of Job's experience. Not the least of this learning is Job's statement in verses five and six:

I have heard of You by the hearing of the ear, but now my eye sees You.

Therefore I abhor myself, and repent in dust and ashes.

Job 42:5,6

Satan certainly set up the arena for Job's experience and problems. But the will of the Father in this instance was more than a simple contest of pride with Satan. There were also ultimate issues of inestimable value at stake for Job himself.

The Accuser of the Brethren: Ourselves

Satan is preeminently an accuser of the believer. This activity has some effect on God, but it is more frequently something which occurs within the believer himself!

The Bible clearly shows that Satan cannot bring the believer to court, as it were, because our faith in the offering of Jesus Christ has forever settled that issue: "There is therefore now no condemnation to those who are in Christ Jesus..." (Romans 8:1).

Satan's accusation, therefore, is an annoying and persistent attack which wearies and frustrates the believer's victory. It could be said that Satan's arena can only exist when we allow it.

If we stand faithfully on the written Word of the Lord, this "stadium" loses its compulsive power over us. No one has discussed this better than C. S. Lewis in his amazing book, *The Screwtape Letters.*

The fictional letters satirize the routine of hell to try to trip up believers. Their most successful tactic was to get Christians to dwell on one or all of their failures. If a Christian could be made to feel guilty about his performance in the Christian life, his effectiveness was eliminated.

Satan's Six Psychological Tools

Dr. James Dobson, eminent professor of pediatrics and world-renowned psychologist, once listed six psychological tools which Satan uses in warfare against believers.

The first five include: (1) fear and anxiety, (2) unforgivable guilt, (3) doubt and pessimism, (4) anger and hostility, and (5) fatigue.

But Dr. Dobson's sixth tool, which he said was head and shoulders above all the others, attracted my attention the most. He describes this sixth psychological tool of Satan as "widespread, deep-seated feelings of inferiority and inadequacy."

Before you dismiss that too quickly, you need to understand that those nagging self-doubts, those bitter disappointments of who or what we are, are the *only* possibility of Satan's really dragging us into an arena of conflict.

Dr. Dobson went on in this message to say that Satan uses these feelings of inadequacy to do the following:

1. to paralyze and immobilize us

2. to contaminate our relationship with God

3. to impose conformity upon us

4. to isolate us from other people

In each instance, the believer would be taken away from meaningful and significant purpose, intimacy, and relationship. *Feelings of inadequacy are enforced by unfounded comparisons with others, and are always debilitating.*

For we dare not class ourselves or compare ourselves with those who commend themselves. But they, measuring themselves by themselves, and comparing themselves among themselves, are not wise.

2 Corinthians 10:12

Satan's Pattern Revealed

There is an incredibly revealing story in the Old Testament which unveils the manner of Satan's arena of problems for the believer. It concerns the restoration period of Israel following the seventy-year captivity.

The context of the story is the description of the initial project of the restoration, the rebuilding of the Temple. Although the returning refugees had begun to build with fervor and joy, the project was soon abandoned.

There were subtle and open attacks from surrounding enemies, including appeals to various changing world powers. But, more importantly, there had come a sense of futility and hopelessness among the restorers themselves.

The Temple would never possess its former glory, they concluded — and some even wept over the attempt to rebuild it. Satan knows how to use discouragement, disappointment, and failure to bring an abandonment of Christian purpose and victory.

The Role of Sin and Guilt

There had also been sin in an unfortunate leadership decision to allow the people to intermarry with the people of the land, since the returnees were limited in number.

The ramifications of sin and guilt are no small part of the believer's vulnerability to the enemy. And, to be frank, there are limited resources among this tattered band, and they really did seem more like pawns in the ever-changing game of world politics.

The result was that for approximately sixteen years the uncompleted Temple was a mocking charade to the purposes of God. We are reminded of Jesus' message on discipleship that we must sit down first and "count the cost" (Luke 14:28).

Finally, aged Haggai began remonstrating the people toward completing the project. He inspired a much younger and brighter prophet, captive born, to begin prophesying. His name was Zechariah, and on one January night, God gave him eight visions which addressed all the major causes of the work's disruption.

Central to these visions was one of the young High Priest, Joshua, standing before the Lord in excrement-bespattered garments, and Satan standing at his right hand to condemn and oppose him (Zechariah 3).

Sixteen Years of Ineffectiveness

If you understand the background, you immediately understand what this represents. Here stands Joshua, head bent, hearing the accusation, caught in a verbal tennis match, debilitated by conscience, ineffective through guilt, and unable or unwilling to receive God's verdict. Do you see? Here stands sixteen years of immobilization and ineffectiveness!

The vision of Zechariah shows us that the Lord rebukes and perpetually rebukes Satan, saying, in essence, that He chooses and continues to choose Jerusalem.

He sees Joshua's weaknesses, but He also understands the reason. "Is this not a brand plucked from the fire?" He inquires (Zechariah 3:2).

Issuing a command, the High Priest's filthy robes are stripped away and replaced with rich robes, including, at Zechariah's suggestion, a clean turban representing restored authority.

"Hooray! you say. "The good guys win!" But is this really true?

Satan can never bring a believer to a literal place of *judgment*. However, he wins by our agreement to be hauled to such a place of *accusation* and *condemnation*. In a sense, just standing there, Satan has already won, although technically he is defeated.

The Consequence of Devastating Introspection

To keep Joshua at this place, Satan has stopped the program. Devastating introspection has blocked the ministry for sixteen long years. Satan's only hope is to stop you short of the purposes of God for your life. He has no other authority.

His only tools are what we give him. Our cooperation is *mandatory* for his effectiveness. No wonder one of the great shouts of the redeemed in heaven is when "...the accuser of our brethren, who accused them before our God day and night, has been cast down" (Revelation 12:10).

CHAPTER 13

Strategy For Triumph

Most hotels or apartment buildings will not show a thirteenth floor in their buildings. That floor becomes the fourteenth because of the superstitious fears of the patrons. Nonetheless, we must conclude our study with a thirteenth chapter.

Thirteen in the Bible can sometimes be a number symbolizing rebellion and disobedience. A careful scrutiny, however, will show that the number thirteen often shows how God replaces those who are unwilling to walk in His full purpose. The tribes of Israel and the disciples are cases in point.

The number can, therefore, mean God's grace among us to complete His original plan and to fill up His purposes. That seems most appropriate to our study of *Strategy for Triumph.*

Since six is the biblical number of man, and seven is the number of spiritual perfection and completion, I like to consider thirteen as a combination of God's perfect righteousness and completion upon all our humanity. That is certainly my prayer, at any rate, as we conclude this book.

The believer experiences problems because the nature and the essence of the Christian experience is change and pilgrimage. We are being conformed to the image or likeness of Jesus Christ, and the change is occurring from glory or significance unto glory or significance (2 Corinthians 3:18).

The Good News About Change

Change itself is a difficult and challenging arena. But there is good news: The change has a purpose, and we will ultimately be pleased with the result!

I was told that the great sculptor Michelangelo, argued with a stone mason on one occasion over a particularly odd-shaped piece of rock. Apparently this piece, which was leaning against the quartz stock, was left over from a major granite cut. It was long and extremely narrow, and it was destined to be cut into smaller pieces.

Michelangelo, however, wanted it as it was. He saw something in it he had been looking for. Rushing to his studio with it, he began bringing forth from the stone the angular form of the adolescent David.

Supposedly the great sculptor worked with less than a quarter inch of error-space or tolerance on either side — and that's really cutting it close!

"Brands Plucked From the Fire"

No man calls himself to be a Christian. It is the selection and work of the Holy Spirit which bring us individually to the point of conversion and revelation, which then result in our becoming a new creation in Jesus Christ.

As with the young High Priest we saw in the last chapter, God sees each of us, in a sense, as brands which have been "plucked from the fire."

There is a great deal of work to be done in every believer if the likeness of Jesus Christ is to surface from the rough stone of our lives!

The believer must, therefore, maintain a certain divine flexibility, setting forth on a great adventure, leaving the known and the secure, and reaching for the vision which will challenge and change his life. Whatever else is to be said, the Christian life is not meant to be boring!

We have seen that problems are really the means of propelling us forward! Another way of stating this is that problems are opportunities for change in our life.

Whether or not we are candidates for the rushing stream of change in life, marriage, stewardship, ministry, and discipline is an entirely different question.

Nurturing Holy Dissatisfaction

There must be a holy dissatisfaction within us like that of the English bishop who once despaired, "Everywhere the Apostle Paul went, there was a riot. Everywhere I go, they serve tea!"

The Holy Spirit is "the divine coach of change," and the Bible is the preeminent change literature of all time. Our problems, their sources and arenas, are true "change-settings" for our life.

Perhaps there is a mega- or macro-change intended, or perhaps it is only adjustment through a micro-change. But, like a frustrated suitor viewing his date, the Holy Spirit must surely say of us, "*Any* change is an improvement!"

Guidance and Change

Acts 16 shows us such an example when twice the Holy Spirit attempts to stop a well-meaning but wrong trip by Paul and his team to Asia, or Bithynia (Acts 16:6,7).

The arena of this change involved a severe break in relationship between Paul and Barnabas (Acts 15:36-39), and probably physical illness.

Guidance and change generally come through circumstances — commonplace things, difficult and disappointing things. Problems become the context for change and, therefore, for release, advance, and growth.

The planned trip to Asia Minor was supposed to been no more than a Sunday stroll through the park. Paul's intention was, simply, "Let us now go back and visit our brethren in every city where we have preached the word of the Lord, and see how they are doing" (Acts 15:36).

However, because of the problems in Acts 16 and the resulting redirection of the Lord, it became the Apostle Paul's most dramatic involvement in the harvest! Philippi, Athens, Corinth, and Thessalonica were all to be the result of God's change for the apostle and his time in this instance!

A Theory of History

A great contemporary writer, Malachi Martin, postulates an interesting "trap gate" theory of history in his amazing Vatican history, *Three Popes and a Cardinal*. Basically, he suggests that we should best understand the events and changes of life and our world if we could consider history running like water through a time-linear pipe.

Periodically, there are check valves or trap gates which prevent the unimpeded continuation of things as they are. Cultures and peoples pass through such check gates, and they are never able to return.

Can't you see you own experience in that illustration? I certainly can. There have been many such moments in my life when God has arranged or allowed a situation which forever altered the direction of my life.

Tragically, many people stand at these trap gates trying to drag through them and into the new, things from the old that were meant to be left behind!

Checkpoints for Change

How, then, should you view the arena of problems and change that begins building around you? Perhaps you are frustrated, confused, and uncertain about the purpose or even the source of the circumstances. Let me suggest these three important checkpoints at such a moment.

1. Recommit to your position as a servant-disciple of Jesus Christ.

To be a Christian means to belong to the Lord. We are Christ's servants, being conformed to His likeness. Whether or not you are comfortable or happy about the circumstances, ask not *where* they've come from, but *why* they're there!

Nothing comes that I can't learn from, grow by, or experience something from. We live in a fallen world, so my circumstances are not always to be taken simply as "God's will." They can, in any event, be an occasion for God's glory to be made perfect in my weakness.

2. *Carefully evaluate the situation, using every fact or understanding you can gather to gain a true perspective of your situation.*

In Acts 16, after the frustrating "no" from God through circumstances, Paul had a vision of a Macedonian, or European man, asking for help.

And after he had seen the vision, immediately we sought to go to Macedonia, concluding [assuredly gathering] **that the Lord had called us to preach the gospel to them.**

Acts 16:10

The word "concluding" here is the Greek *sumbibazo,* which literally means "to lay things together." It's very helpful at critical moments of problem and change to sit down quietly and review the facts. Try to unite or drive together pieces of the circumstances as you see them. And notice the "we" of this passage.

Often the counsel of close Christian friends will help us to perceive what is actually happening, apart from the more careless and presumptuous evaluation of what "seems" to be happening.

3. *Learn to submit quickly — immediately — to the process.*

Your evaluation may have revealed sin which needs to be repented of and forgiven. Perhaps there are obvious and specific changes that need to be made. Obey quickly!

Delayed obedience is disobedience. Besides, the sooner the lesson is learned, the change made, the arena of the problem can be ended!

Leaping Into the Muddy Jordan

There is an interesting parable for us in the story of Naaman, the Syrian general and leper. You remember that a maid had told him of help that was available through her country and her faith.

But when Naaman was sent from king to prophet, and finally was greeted by a *servant*, it was about all he could take. What's more, the instruction to bathe seven times in the muddy Jordan was totally unacceptable!

The Bible says Naaman became furious, and went away and said to himself:

He will surely come out to me, and stand and call on the name of the Lord his God, and wave his hand over the place, and heal the leprosy.

2 Kings 5:11

It's dangerous to have prearranged concepts of how or what God will do!

Naaman almost kept his leprosy rather than descend to the direction of God's purpose. He had a great problem with how the word or purpose of God came to him, and what the method of God entailed. To be truthful, *so do we!*

"Couldn't I learn this lesson some other way?" we ask. "Can't I write the curriculum, or design the manner of the experience?" We think we could better accomplish the purpose through our own method.

"Are not the Abanah and the Pharpar, the rivers of Damascus, better than all the waters of Israel?" Naaman insisted. "Could I not wash in them and be clean?" (2 Kings 5:12). He turned and walked away in a rage.

Our problems are often to us what the Jordan was to Naaman: an unacceptable alternative. But God has a method in having us descend into the rhythm of His purpose.

Thank God, Naaman's servant persuaded him, and he went down to the Jordan, dipped seven times, "...and his flesh was restored like the flesh of a little child, and he was clean" (verse 14).

The Challenge: Change Your Attitude

Perhaps this book is like a sensible servant to you. It bids you confront your Christian experience with a different attitude, and thus change and develop into the purposes of God for your life.

We've certainly tried to deal with the Word and the way of God. One thing is predictable: When we yield to God's way, we come quickly into what He purposed, and what we inwardly need and long for.

After the early missionaries in Acts 16 discovered the reason for the delays and problems, and turned their focus to the direction of the Holy Spirit, the Word says: "Therefore, sailing from Troas, we ran a straight course to Samothrace, and the next day came to Neapolis..." (Acts 16:11).

That verse begins a paragraph which gives us the first page in the history of everything which resulted in Europe, from the strange method of the Holy Spirit preventing, hindering, and guiding Paul.

Sailing "A Straight Course"

Particularly note in verse 11 the idiomatic narrative phrase which is translated "a straight course." It literally was understood in the New Testament to mean, "*sailing* before the wind." Later on, in Acts 20, the identical journey — the same voyage — occupied five days with a contrary wind!

The sailor's warm dream is to sail with the tide and before the wind. The wind of the Christian experience is the Holy Spirit, who blows where He chooses (John 3:8).

My prayer for you is that you quickly hoist your sail in the direction of His movement, and come quickly and with minimum resistance into His safe port of progress, growth, and Christ-likeness.

Here's to good sailing with favorable winds!

Recommended Reading List

I began this book by saying that there are no simple answers to most Christian dilemmas, and that books do not reveal infallible formulas. The following suggestions are not a bibliography of subjects, but the personal introduction to a well-worn and intimate circle of friends.

These books weren't chosen because they're impressive or particularly contemporary, but because they've influenced me, and I more delight in your possible fellowship with the authors than in any particular dogma.

* * *

These old-timers will speak to you regularly. Get anything you find which they've written.

Tozer, A. W., *The Pursuit of God.*

Hession, Roy and Revel, *The Calvary Road.* Christian Literature Crusade.

Simpson, A. B., *The Self Life and The Christ Life.*

Murray, Andrew, *Absolute Surrender.*

Chambers, Oswald, *My Utmost for His Highest.*

Chambers, Oswald, *Bringing Sons Unto Glory.*

Paxson, Ruth, *Life on the Highest Plane.* Baker Book House.

* * *

Prayer is so important, so personal, but you need encouragement, not condemnation.

Eastman, Dick, *No Easy Road*. Baker Book House.

Bounds, E. M., *Power Through Prayer*. Zondervan.

Torrey, R. A., *The Power of Prayer*. Zondervan.

Hayford, Jack, *Prayer Is Invading the Impossible*. Ballantine.

Tompkins, Iverna, *God and I*. Logos International.

* * *

Discipleship is a relationship.

Sanders, J. Oswald, *Problems of Christian Discipleship*. Lutterworth Press.

Bonhoeffer, Dietrich, *The Cost of Discipleship*. The Macmillan Company.

MacDonald, Gordon, *Ordering Your Private World*. Thomas Nelson Inc.

Baxter, J. Sedlow, *Going Deeper*. Zondervan.

Torrey, R. A., *The Holy Spirit*. Fleming H. Revell.

McClury, Floyd Sr., *The Father Heart of God*. Harvest House.

Cunningham, Loren, *Is That Really You, God?* Chosen Books.

Elliot, Elizabeth, *Shadow of the Almighty*. Harper & Brothers.

* * *

A real *Koinonia* group.

Larson, Bruce, *Living on the Growing Edge*.

Larson, Bruce, *Ask Me To Dance*.

Larson, Bruce, *No Longer Strangers*.

Frost, Robert C., *Aglow With the Spirit*.

Schaeffer, Francis A., *Escape From Reason*. Intervarsity Press.

Muggeridge, Malcolm, *A Third Testament*. Ballantine Books.

Wilkerson, David, *The Cross and the Switchblade*.

Tournier, Paul, *The Whole Person in a Broken World* (and anything else). Harper & Row.

Nee, Watchman, *The Normal Christian Life.* Christian Literature Crusade.

Lindsey, Hal, *Satan Is Alive and Well on Planet Earth.* Zondervan.

Paulk, Earl, *The Wounded Body of Christ.*

Pippert, Rebecca M., *Out of the Saltshaker.* Intervarsity Press.

Ogilvie, Lloyd John, *A Life Full of Surprises* (and anything else). Abingdon Press.

* * *

And we like our own work.

Howard, Rick C., *Tents, Temples and Palaces,* an Old Testament survey study. International Correspondence Institute.

Howard, Rick C., *Christian Maturity,* a personal study book. International Correspondence Institute.

Howard, Rick C., *The Judgment Seat of Christ.* Naioth Sound & Publishing.

Howard, Rick C., *Tape Catalog,* a complete catalog of the preaching ministry of Rick C. Howard. Naioth Sound & Publishing.

All the above materials by Rick C. Howard are available through Naioth Sound & Publishing, 2995 Woodside Road, Suite 400, Woodside, CA 94062; 1-800-368-3827

To order books and tapes by
Rick Howard,
or to contact him for speaking engagements,
please write or call:

Naioth Sound and Publishing
2995 Woodside Road, Suite 400
Woodside, CA 94062
1-800-368-3827